D0780445

STORAGE

We Won't Pay! We Won't Pay!

A POLITICAL FARCE

by Dario Fo

North American version by R.G. Davis

8418

SAMUEL FRENCH, INC.

45 WEST 25TH STREET   NEW YORK 10010
7623 SUNSET BOULEVARD   HOLLYWOOD 90046
LONDON   *TORONTO*

EDITORIAL NOTE
by Dario Fo

The Latin peoples called actors "histriones." In the Lombard dialect "strion" means magician or seer. And so in our text, we too have disguised ourselves as "histrion/seers" and have gone in for prophecy. But not by means of a cabal. On the contrary, attempting to apply logic. First, an examination of the facts, then the development of the results of analysis into a fundamentally Marxist practice.

But is it possible to create a farce using "the philosophy of practice?" I know that such an idea would make the serious and pedantic intellectuals of our Marxist doctrine shudder. But we of La Commune are not "serious" Marxists. In fact, we are a mass of "villains" and, like all villains of this world, we enjoy smiling and mockery, being grotesque, vulgar and at times, scurrilous.

In fact, "scurre" was the epithet that the bishops hurled at the popular jesters (Volgari) as far back as the 4th Century A.D., and we feel quite at home with that bunch. Mao said: ". . . without faith; always in doubt; not only for destruction, but for construction. Because our only faith is in reason."

We are convinced that in laughter, in the grotesque of satire, exists the maximum expression of doubt, the most valid support of reason.

Accordingly, we have chosen the farce as the instrument of our work as actors in service to the class war because it is the theatrical form invented by the people ". . . to cut with the scorching tongue and inexorable putrid pit into which the ruling class is splattered." That putrid pit is the bourgeois culture.

But let us return to WE WON'T PAY! WE WON'T

3

PAY!: this farce was written a few months ago in the summer of 1974. At the time, there was talk of an imminent crisis, of upcoming working class struggles over the cost of living, of entire factories placed on unemployment.

In writing this comedy, we wanted to play with fantasy to an excess. We had previsions which at that time (now more than three months ago) seemed like fantasy-politics. But then reality not only copied us but surpassed us by leaps and bounds.

We foresaw that the ruling class would attack the working class with maximum cynicism and violence in an attempt to bring the working class to its knees; that the "entrepreneurs" would artfully inflate the economic crisis in order to blackmail the government; that the most powerful ministers of government, even those in the bourgeois parties would be capable of nothing but banging their heads against the wall.

We foresaw that the working class, the people of the ghetto, would react by organizing self-reduction of gas, electricity, and rent bills, and would develop another great invention of the proletarian struggle: to go shopping in the supermarket and impose just prices. On the other hand, seeing that the boss attacks you by taking away two, three, four days of work a week, how do you combat him? "The strike is no longer enough," say the workers. "In fact, in a certain way, in striking you do the boss a favor because in this way he doesn't pay you anymore, not even unemployment; and then you still have to carry his load on your back." That "load" is precisely the merchandise that the worker produces and that the boss resells or rents to you until you choke: home, gas, electricity, commuter passes, food: in short, life.

We have recounted the story of two working class families who bestir themselves to fight using the weapon of "civil disobedience." And through conflicts and polemics we come to understand the value of this new method of striking. A strike where this time, finally, the boss pays and only him.

As in the old Neapolitan and Venetian popular farces (it would be better to say ancient) the mainspring, the key at the bottom, is hunger. The initial solution, the instinct to look out for one's own, attempts to resolve the ancestral problem of the appetite. It then transforms into a need to operate collectively, to organize and fight united; not to arrive at mere survival, but to truly live ". . . in a world, maybe with fewer shiny store windows and freeways . . . but with fewer corrupt bureaucrats in the government, too—and fewer crooks, the big, fat ones, the real crooks and with justice, with justice, by God!"

"Where we who have always slaved to support them all, would finally start supporting ourselves, building our own homes, creating a life for ourselves! A way of living that lets us be happy! Where the desire to laugh comes forth as if it were a fiesta . . . the desire to play and to celebrate . . . and even to be happy working . . . like human men and women, not stupid animals . . . without joy or imagination . . . A world where you can notice that there is a sky . . . that plants and trees flower, that there is springtime . . . that girls laugh and sing . . . And at the end, when you die, it wasn't just an old mule that dropped dead, no! it was a human being that died; one who lived happy and free . . . along with other free people!"

In following these developments, we wish to avoid falling into ideological didacticism, so we have sought to resolve them in a theatre of "situation." That is, in a mode tied to the "epic" theatre, where it is not the characters who move the scenes forward, but the situation, the theatrical engine.

The facts determine the plot and start it; and the characters, involved from the situation that one created are the gears that move and make the engine function. One lever releases a mechanism at times paradoxical, which enlarges it like a pantograph, redoubles it, turns it over, accelerates it, explodes it into motion.

But this is not a choice of "occupation" even if the occupation under these circumstances and in this theatrical genre is a cultural choice, because to create a theatre of situation means to represent a story and not to recite it. It means to not be preoccupied with the "drama" borne of the individual character's private problems in his rapport with others; but on the contrary, it is borne of everyone's problems that explode in a dialectical conflict from the "situation" of their rapport with one another. It is the problem of the "us" (collective) against the "I" (of individualism).

We present an opposing way of understanding culture and therefore, the theatre. A theatre of the classes but not interclassist. You have probably noted in speaking of theatrical structures the repeated and continuous "we" thought, "we" chose, etc. In truth, the drafting of textual material is accountable to me alone; but from the first improvisational rehearsal to the staging, the text has been discussed countless times, not only within the collective, but more importantly, with groups of workers and vanguards from the various factories in Milan, presented many times to these gatherings before actually setting the script. As a result of these discussions, we recognized holes in the text, scenes that had to be developed differently. The truly constructive criticism of our comrades convinced us to change and rewrite the entire ending. In our opinion, this is a correct way of creating a "collective" theatre.

Dario Fo

On the Translation

The life of this play under the phrase "North American Version by R.G. Davis" has some interesting turns.

The play was first performed in 1974 in Milan under the title Non Si Paga! Non Si Paga! by Dario's La Commune. Then we found a British version published by Pluto Press called, We Can't Pay, We Won't Pay, based on performances of the Half Moon Theatre Company in London. I saw a video taped version in West Berlin by a Hamburg Company in 1978 called Bezhalt Wird Nicht! Then we did a reading of our first version of a translation by Suzanne and Jim Cowan at the Whole Theater Company in New Jersey June 5, 1979. Chris Silva was dramaturg and Peter Brosius assisted. Another review of the translation was done by Margaret Kunzle in Milan before we received our "official translation" acceptable to Dario Fo and La Commune correspondent Piero Sciotto. But we reviewed that version one more time comparing the Italian to the English. As part of my second year directors teaching contract at NYU 79-80, I was called upon to direct a project with graduate acting students there and so we did the first act of We Won't Pay! We Won't Pay! (Joe Siravo added a translation of Fo's introduction and re-translated lines in the text), which was also performed at Town Hall in New York as part of a support demonstration to protest the U.S. State Department's denial of a visa for Fo and his wife, Franca Rame. (Both of them had been invited to perform in New York City and again in 1983). Next we did the Canadian Premiere and a full professional production at Tamahnous Theatre in Vancouver B.C. which opened Sept 12, 1980. In that production another treatment of the text was executed by Bonnie Borenstien, who was the assistant director for the Vancouver show. On December 16, 1980 we opened the off-Broadway show in New York at the Chelsea Theatre Center with Borenstein again assisting the direction. After 3 and half months the New York production closed on March 29, 1981. Many productions of this text have occurred since that time — additions in "translation" and help on the text have also come from Grubb Grabner and Joe Spano, plus various actors and even typists.

This volume is dedicated to Piero Sciotto, the singing entrepreneur, whose support made this whole project possible.

PRODUCTION SUGGESTIONS
R.G. Davis

It has been my experience that too often directors are underprepared to begin rehearsals. Let us say it is because the commerce of theatre, arrangements made at the last moment, cause the director to skip over a period of learning and reflection.

Toward informing the director, or directors or production team, herein follow a few thoughts derived from my experience with three different Dario Fo plays over a period of three years, directing seven different productions:

The ground base of Dario Fo's style/technique performance is storytelling (Cantastorie). Interestingly, this base is a popular form, closer to performance than acting, and somewhere between the acting styles of Stanislavski and Brecht.

Note in the text of WE WON'T PAY! WE WON'T PAY! that each character, beginning with the long story of Antonia, tells and retells stories. Giovanni not only tells his own stories to Antonia, but retells Antonia's stories to Luigi, thereby summing up the first act in the last scene of that act. Storytelling ability is not Story Theatre; it is another entity and can be learned from folk tellers and children's storytellers (these are usually librarians who read or tell stories to children — some without being cute). The first act relies on storytelling techniques.

The second act is a Vaudeville turn, performed on the ramp and in the style of Vaudeville, like Weber and Fields, Gallagher and Sheen, et al. The stories are still there, the style being shifted a bit.

In the Dario Fo/Franca Rame production that I was

able to see on video cassette, they used a ground plan in a flat, or two-dimensional way, with hardly any naturalistic elements. The wardrobe and the furniture were real, but the placing of the furniture didn't follow the placement in a conventional apartment. (In this production, incidentally, Fo played Giovanni and Rame played Antonia.) The setting was "spare," and details were minimal; no real food was used in the real boxes and jars, for example. I've seen productions with very elaborate settings and lots of "Italian flavor," but I think stage business can distract from the material, and I have opted to keep the junk off the stage in order to create that ambience with only the story, the actors, and essential props.

One of the problems particular to this play lies in keeping the farce elements from overriding the social insights. Another is in keeping the social insights from becoming too heavy-handed, sans humor. Too often these elements are separated, the balance broken by emphasizing one to the detriment of the other. In many cases, when directors look at this material they're annoyed at the politics, or ignorant of them, and the balance is bungled. Try to find the politics in the comedy and the humor in the politics.

Dario Fo is not an anti-Communist, but he does argue for rank and file spontaneous activity rather than conservative party growth. (This debate between the two modes continues in unions and parties, then as now.) It is essential that the production team read material or be advised by people who know the political underpinnings and arguments of each of the characters. As members of a trade union and the Communist Party, these people struggle for a way to improve their lives. In a country where two million people are members of the

Party (begun in Italy in 1921), whose record in the fight against fascism is commendable, it's all just a little distant from our usual personal experiences at home in North America. One does not need to be a Communist to play these roles, yet, just as any actor would learn something about iambic pentameter in preparation for Shakespeare, or southern sexual mores for Tennessee Williams, then one must understand the theories and political arguments that these working people live, fight and laugh over.

This is not a message play; it is written from a particular view like all plays. Fo, a Marxist, views social problems from that perspective. Antonia is no feminist and Giovanni is no dumb-dumb. The contradictions posed will not be solved in the theatre. The play demonstrates ways of looking at living conditions.

CHELSEA THEATER CENTER

DOWNSTAIRS THEATER

Robert Kalfin, Producing Director
A. Harrison Cromer, Managing Director

LEAVIN/DAVIS PRODUCTIONS
in association with **Chris Silva** and
Chelsea Theater Center

present

WE WON'T PAY!
WE WON'T PAY!

by
DARIO FO

*North American Translation
and
Direction by*
R. G. DAVIS

Production Design by
WOLFGANG ROTH

Featuring

| KAREN SHALLO | | HARRIS LASKAWY |
| BONNIE BRAELOW | ROBERT DeFRANK | W. T. MARTIN |

Costume Design by
DENISE ROMANO

Light & Sound Design by
TERRY ALAN SMITH

Production Stage Manager
WM. HARE

First public performance, New York City, December 2, 1980

This production is made possible in part with public funds from the New York State Council on the Arts and the National Endowment for the Arts.

14

PROLOGUE

(All-purpose actor, posing as Italian Tourist Agent,
in front of Stage or on Apron)

Buona serra, signor e signorini. I welcome you to
*NON SI PAGA, NON SI PAGA, WE WON'T PAY!
WE WON'T PAY!* My name is Fulvio Bardi. I am from
the Italian tourist bureau and I have been asked by the
producers of this show, because it is an Italian play, to
speak to you about Italy and to encourage you to visit
our beautiful country. This play takes place in Milano, a
very beautiful and very famous city in the north of my
country, where one can take part in a very active
cultural life ... of that city. The characters of this play
live in a working class neighborhood, but like
neighborhoods in your country, you drive through, you
wouldn't even notice. But you go to another neighborhood, you see we drive the Ferraris, we wear the Gucci
shoes, like the film stars: Marcello Mastroianni, Gian-
carlo Gianini, Sophia Loren—who we hope will return
to Italy after she has straightened out her taxes—and,
the author of this play, Dario Fo.

Although we are not sure Dario Fo wears the Gucci
shoes, he is known in Italy as a famous TV star, and
throughout Europe as a virtuoso performer. He was going to be here tonight, but, unfortunately, he was denied
a visa by your state department ... a minor foul-up ...
which we are sure with your new president, Renaldo
Reagan, who will be more sympathetic with the artist,
will be solved in no time. You know that it is a great
mis-conception to think that Dario Fo's politics have
anything to do with his plays. He is first and primemost
an artist. As we all know, art and politics do not mix
like oil and water. This play is a work of art, and like all
works of art, like Monet's "The Water Lilies" for instance, it is a reflection of ... of ... water.

15

Now the characters in this play are members of the Communist Party, but we do not want you to get from that that this is a political play, because in Italy our communists are nice communists and they make up one third of the vote. Actually, we are quite conservative. We share borders with France and Greece which are socialist, and with Yugoslavia which is communist. As you know, we are still ruled by the Masonic Lodge.

But if there should occur something in the play which you find too political, I suggest that you make use of an age-old Italian custom. Allow me to demonstrate: if you don't like what you hear, you put your hands like this (over ears). If you don't like what you see, you put your hands like this (over eyes). And if you don't like what you see and what you hear, you don't want to get involved, you raise your hands like this (Fuck-you gesture). Please feel free to practice that at any time during the show. Perhaps you would all like to practice a little before we start. You don't like what you hear . . . (ad lib practice).

We know that you will enjoy the show, and, remember, if you are planning a trip to Italy, be sure to see me at intermission or after the show and I will be happy to help you with anything but airline reservations. In sympathy with your air traffic controllers' strike, the controllers in my country have decided to show up for work and it is a very dangerous situation. For those of you undecided about visiting my country, I brought a brochure. This one is for . . . (improvisation off brochure).

There are many tours available. One of the more popular in this part of the country is "The Mediterranean Sea: Cradle of Civilization and Home of the Fruit Fly." For those of you of the Catholic faith, there is the

"Cardinal Cody Tour," with all expenses paid for single women over seventy.

I only brought one of these, so I will give it to you, and you can pass it around, always remembering the words of that great French Marxist, Alexander Dumas: "All for one and one for all."

Have a good evening, and ciao.

We Won't Pay!
We Won't Pay!

ACT I

A modest working class apartment. To the right, a ta-
ble; a cupboard, a refrigerator, a gas range, and,
close by, two gas tanks hooked up for welding.
Along one wall, a daybed and a wardrobe.
A woman, ANTONIA, enters, followed by a younger
woman, MARGHERITA. They are loaded with
shopping bags, filled to overflowing, and with dif-
ferent plastic bags stuffed with goods, which they
place on the table and daybed.

ANTONIA. It's really lucky that I ran into you today
. . . If not, I really don't know how I'd have managed to
drag all this stuff here.

MARGHERITA. But where did you find the money to
buy all this stuff?

ANTONIA. I told you, I didn't buy it, I won it with
green stamps . . . and then, in a box of laundry powder,
I found a prize. I happened to find a gold coin . . .

MARGHERITA. Sure, go tell that to someone else . . . a
gold coin, c'mon!

ANTONIA. You don't believe my story?

MARGHERITA. Of course not!

ANTONIA. Okay, then, I'll tell you another one.

MARGHERITA. Ciao.

ANTONIA. Where are you going?

MARGHERITA. See ya!

ANTONIA. No, no, hold on, I'll tell you the truth.

19

MARGHERITA. (*rushes to sit*) Okay, tell me.

ANTONIA. Well, I went to the supermarket, and there was a bunch of women and a few men, too, raising hell over the prices going up so much that it's enough to make you sick.

MARGHERITA. You said it, enough to make you sick!!

ANTONIA. Pasta and sugar, it's awful not to mention meat and canned goods . . . And there was the manager, trying to calm us down: "It's not my fault," he kept saying, "it's management that sets the prices . . . and they've decided to raise them." Decided? With whose permission? "With nobody's permission, it's legal; that's free enterprise, free competition!" Free competition, against who? Against us? And we're supposed to take it? Your money or your life! You're a bunch of thieves — I yelled that myself, and then hid.

MARGHERITA. Good for you!

ANTONIA. Then one woman said, "We've had it! Basta! This time *we're* setting the prices. We'll only pay the same as last year. And if you object, we'll take the stuff away without paying at all. Got it? Take it or leave it!" You should have seen him: the manager went white as a sheet. "But you're all crazy! I'm calling the police!" So he shoots like a rocket over to the checkout counter to telephone . . . but the telephone isn't working; somebody has cut the wire. "Excuse me, let me get to my office, excuse me!" But he couldn't get through . . . all those women around him . . . he starts pushing and one woman pretends that she's hit . . . she makes like she'd just passed out.

MARGHERITA. Oh, beautiful! Che bello!

ANTONIA. Then a great big fat woman started hollering, "You coward! You picked on a poor woman . . . who's probably pregnant, too! If she loses the baby, you'll see what'll happen to you! We'll send you to jail! Murderer!" Then everybody yelled: "Baby killer!" "Baby killer!" "Baby killer!"

MARGHERITA. Oh, I wish I'd been there.

ANTONIA. Yeah, it was quite a sight.

MARGHERITA. And then what happened?

ANTONIA. Well, it happened that that fool of a manager . . . completely terrified . . . gave in . . . and we paid what we'd wanted to. I must say that one woman overdid it; she wanted to take the stuff on credit, and wouldn't give her name. "I can't tell you where I live," she said, "because you're liable to turn me in to the police . . . I know you guys! You'll just have to put your faith in trust. Trust is the soul of business . . . don't you always say that? Well, Arriverderci! Trust me!"

MARGHERITA. Oh, boy!

ANTONIA. Then someone started yelling: "The police!" It was a false alarm, but everybody took off . . . some dropped their packages, others burst out crying they were so scared. Then these workers from the factory near there . . . started saying, "Calma, calma! What's all this chickenshit, why be afraid of the police? For god's sake! You're right to pay what's fair! Hey, this is a strike, in fact, better, because in a strike the workers always lose money . . . and now this is a strike where the boss loses out!" "We women can even go one better: We won't pay! We won't pay! And that goes for all the money you've been stealing from us in the years we've been coming here to shop!" So I made up my mind and did my shopping all over again. I was yelling: "We won't pay! We won't pay!" And all the other women too: "We won't pay! We won't pay!" It was like the storming of the Bastille!

MARGHERITA. Beautiful!

ANTONIA. Yeah, it was really like a party, but not so much because we didn't pay for the stuff, but because we suddenly found ourselves all together, men and women, doing something really right and brave against those crooks. We really caught 'em off balance! Now they're beginning to get scared, and in some super-markets they've already brought down the prices.

MARGHERITA. Sure, you all did great, but now what are you going to tell your husband? You're not gonna feed him that story about the green stamps, are you?

ANTONIA. You don't think he'll swallow it?

MARGHERITA. Of course not.

ANTONIA. Well, maybe it is a bit far-fetched. Trouble is, he's such a law-abiding citizen he'll shit a brick. I ran out of money today so tomorrow I won't have a cent for the gas and electricity. At least I don't worry about the rent. I haven't paid it for four months!

MARGHERITA. Well, for that matter, I don't have any money left either! And *I* haven't paid the rent for *five* months! And I didn't even manage to go shopping like you did today ...

ANTONIA. Now, to start with, we have to hide everything. Do me a favor and take some of this stuff yourself. (*gives her a sack*)

MARGHERITA. No, no, really, thanks, but I don't want it ... I already told you I haven't got a cent to pay you.

ANTONIA. Look, don't be silly. It's gift merchandise! Today we're giving credit!

MARGHERITA. Sure, and then what am I gonna tell my husband? "Look, this stuff is only half-stolen!" He'll half kill me!

ANTONIA. Mine won't; he won't kill me, but he'll drive me nuts with his ranting and raving ... he'll bring up the honor of his sullied name ... "Better to drop dead from hunger than to break the law! I've always paid for everything to the last penny ... Poor, but honest ... Hold my head high among the people," and on and on ... a pain in the ass. But what did I get? (*examines the sack on the table*) What's in this jar? (*reading*) "Reconstituted meat for dogs and cats?" Look! (*She hands the jar to her friend.*)

MARGHERITA. What's this, "Homogenized with different flavors." Why did you get it?

ANTONIA. I really don't know ... I guess in the confusion ... I just grabbed what I found ... And look at this! (*shows a packet*) "Select millet bird seed!"

MARGHERITA. Bird seed?

ANTONIA. Thank goodness it's all stuff I didn't pay for; otherwise I'd be mad. (*shows a box*) Frozen rabbit heads!

MARGHERITA. Come on! Rabbit heads?!

ANTONIA. Well, that's what it says: 'To enrich your chicken feed ... ten heads, two hundred lira!"

MARGHERITA. But that's crazy. And you want me to take this crap home?

ANTONIA. No, not the rabbit heads; I want them. You can take the ordinary stuff: oil, pasta ... Quick, get going! Your husband is working the night shift, you've plenty of time to hide it.

MARGHERITA. Sure, hide it, and then the police come to search the building house by house!

ANTONIA. Don't talk garbage; the police! The whole neighborhood was at the supermarket today ... And there are at least ten thousand families here. (*She goes over and glances out the window.*) Can you imagine the police coming to check us out one by one ... When would they finish up, by Easter? Madonna, my husband! He's coming up; he's already downstairs. Quick, take this stuff. (*She gives her a bag; MARGHERITA moves to leave.*) No, put it under your coat! Help put mine under the bed ... No, don't help me, I'll do it myself. (*MARGHERITA quickly arranges the various bags under her coat and exits. ANTONIA hides all the bags under the bed. Only the one containing the pet food is left out.*) Get going! Get going!

(*GIOVANNI comes in, and runs into MARGHERITA in the doorway.*)

MARGHERITA. Hello, Giovanni!

GIOVANNI. Oh, hi, Margherita ... How's it going?

MARGHERITA. Pretty good, thanks. Ciao, Antonia, see ya' later.

ANTONIA. Yeah, see 'ya later; say hi to your Luigi for me. (*GIOVANNI stands there in confusion, having seen MARGHERITA leaving, with her body all puffed up. ANTONIA takes the plastic bag with the millet, etc., and puts it in the cupboard.*) Well, Giovanni, what are you gaping at? It was about time you got home. Where have you been all this time? (*She starts sweeping, tidying up.*)

GIOVANNI. Hey, what's wrong with Margherita?

ANTONIA. Why, is something wrong with her?

GIOVANNI. She's all big in front, a huge belly!

ANTONIA. Why, is this the first time you've seen a married woman with a big belly before?

GIOVANNI. You mean she's pregnant?

ANTONIA. Well, that's the least that can happen to a woman who has sex.

GIOVANNI. But how far along is she? I saw her just last Sunday, and she didn't seem ...

ANTONIA. Since when have you ever understood anything about women? Last Sunday is a week ago ...

a lot can happen in one week. (*She becomes very busy tidying up the house, but it's clear she's doing all this just to seem nonchalant.*)

GIOVANNI. Listen, I'm not as stupid as that. And anyway her husband, Luigi, didn't tell me about it. We work on the same assembly line, and he always tells me everything about himself and his wife.

ANTONIA. Well, there are—certain things it might bother someone to talk about—

GIOVANNI. What do you mean, bother him? Are you crazy? Why should it bother him to say his wife's pregnant? Are people supposed to be ashamed of having a baby nowadays?

ANTONIA. Well, then, in this case he doesn't know about it yet. And if he doesn't know, how could he go and tell you about it?

GIOVANNI. What do you mean, he doesn't know?

ANTONIA. Well, in this case, she didn't want to tell him.

GIOVANNI. What do you mean she didn't want to tell him?

ANTONIA. Well, Luigi is always going on with Margherita about how it's too soon, it isn't the right moment, we're in the middle of a depression, first they have to get settled . . . and if she gets pregnant, the company she works for will fire her. In fact, he always made her take the pill.

GIOVANNI. And if he made her take the pill, how could she get pregnant?

ANTONIA. Well, in this case the pill didn't work. It happens, you know!

GIOVANNI. But if it happens, why did she keep it a secret from her husband; why should she feel guilty about it?

ANTONIA. Well, in this case, maybe the pill didn't

work because she wasn't taking it. And if you don't take the pill then it happens that the pill doesn't work in this case!

GIOVANNI. What are you talking about?

ANTONIA. Oh, you know she's a real religious Catholic; and since the Pope said, "It's a sin to take the pill" . . .

GIOVANNI. What's the matter, you got rocks in your head. You're talking like a nut; the pill not working because she isn't taking it, the Pope, her looking like she's nine months pregnant and her husband not even noticing?

ANTONIA. But how could he notice it, if she bound herself up?

GIOVANNI. Bound herself up?

ANTONIA. Yeah, wound herself around real tight with bandages so as not to attract attention. In fact, just to-day I told her: "You're crazy, do you want to lose the baby? You're suffocating him. Take off those bandages this minute and who gives a damn if they fire you! The baby is more important!" Did I do the right thing?

GIOVANNI. Sure you did the right thing. Sure!

ANTONIA. Was I good?

GIOVANNI. Sure, sure you were good.

ANTONIA. Well, so then Margherita made up her mind to unwind the bandages and, ploff! her belly popped right out. And then I told her, "If your Luigi starts giving you trouble, tell him to come over here, because my Giovanni is home and he'll straighten him out." Did I do the right thing?

GIOVANNI. Sure you did the right thing.

ANTONIA. Was I good?

GIOVANNI. Yes, yes, sure!

ANTONIA. You hear that, yes, yes, sure . . . what sort of answer is that? Listen, are you mad at me? Come on: what have I done?

GIOVANNI. No, no, I'm not mad at you . . . I'm *mad* because of what happened today in the factory.

ANTONIA. Why, what happened?

GIOVANNI. Well, at lunch time we went down to the cafeteria, and four or five troublemakers began making a stink about the food—saying it was lousy, it was garbage, and all that . . .

ANTONIA. And it really was good stuff—"Excellent food, generous portions". . . ?

GIOVANNI. No, no . . . it was really slop . . . but there was no need to form a mob and raise hell like that!

ANTONIA. What d'ya mean, a mob? You said there were four or five guys!

GIOVANNI. Yeah, at the beginning! But then everybody joined in. They all ate and then walked out without paying.

ANTONIA. Them too?

GIOVANNI. What do you mean, them too?

ANTONIA. Yeah, I mean not only those four or five guys, but everybody else too.

GIOVANNI. Yeah, even the union reps—they should set a good example . . . not join the extremists.

ANTONIA. I'll say!

GIOVANNI. But that's not all; I go out, and on my way to the streetcar I see a whole bunch of women by the supermarket—there must have been a hundred of them shouting, and coming out of the market loaded with stuff. I asked what was going on, and they told me they'd fixed their own prices for the goods! Imagine!

ANTONIA. Ooh, can you beat that!

GIOVANNI. But in fact—they really just took the stuff themselves because most of them walked out without paying!

ANTONIA. Them too?

GIOVANNI. What do you mean, them too?

ANTONIA. Yes, I mean like those troublemakers in your factory who wouldn't pay for the cafeteria meal.

GIOVANNI. That's right, them too. And they even roughed up the manager.

ANTONIA. Which manager, the one in the supermarket or the one in the cafeteria?

GIOVANNI. Both!

ANTONIA. Ooh, can you beat that! I'm just standing here with my mouth hanging open!

GIOVANNI. That's right! Those goddamn ignorant rabble, goddamn provocateurs, goddamned judas pigs who play into the goddamn bosses' hands ... so they can go around saying the workers rip stuff off, calling us a bunch of goddamn crooks ...

ANTONIA. But what do the workers have to do with it? At the supermarket it was the women taking the stuff at cut prices, wasn't it?

GIOVANNI. Yeah, but when they get home, their husbands pretend not to notice anything ... or they even say, "Brava, you did the right thing, stealing stuff." Instead of smashing them over the head with every can and package, one by one. Because "if" my wife pulled something like that, I'd make her eat the tin can along with the little key. So you better not get any bright ideas about stealing, because "if" I ever hear you grabbed stuff at the supermarket without paying, or took a discount on even one can of anchovies, I'll ... I'll ...

ANTONIA. . . . you'll make me eat it along with the little key!

GIOVANNI. No, more than that, I'll leave this house. I'll pack my bags and disappear for good! In fact, first I'll kill you and then I'll file for divorce!

ANTONIA. Listen, if you're going to talk like that, you can leave right now, without waiting for a divorce. How dare you insinuate that I—listen, rather than bring home stuff I haven't paid the legal price for, I'd let you die of starvation!

GIOVANNI. Right, I'd rather you did! And speaking of starvation, what's for supper? With that circus in the cafeteria today, I even missed my lunch. So, what do we eat?

ANTONIA. This! (*She places the two cans of pet food on the table.*)

GIOVANNI. What's this stuff?

ANTONIA. Can't you read? It's special meat by-products for dogs and cats.

GIOVANNI. What?

ANTONIA. It's very good!

GIOVANNI. It may be very good for dogs!

ANTONIA. That's all there was. Besides, it's cheap, "nutritious . . . rich in proteins . . . delicious!" Look, it says so right here!

GIOVANNI. Are you trying to make a fool out of me?

ANTONIA. Who's trying to make a fool out of you? Hey, do you ever go and do the grocery shopping? You know how much they're charging for oil, meat, ham—everything costs twice as much as it used to, and besides, you can't find anything: they're hoarding it all, so they can set up a black market. It's worse than in wartime!

GIOVANNI. Don't exaggerate—wartime! Anyway, I'm not a dog yet ... and I won't do it! I refuse.

ANTONIA. Refuse all you want. Because maybe you're not a dog yet—in fact, you're definitely not—but the boss doesn't see it that way. He thinks we're lower than dogs!

GIOVANNI. OK, OK! Take this crap away. You eat it if it really appeals to you. Look, I'll just have a glass of milk, that'll do.

ANTONIA. I'm sorry, there isn't any milk.

GIOVANNI. What do you mean, there isn't any?

ANTONIA. Oh, don't you know? This morning the milk truck came, and a rumor started that they'd raised the price again ... and then a bunch of troublemakers, irresponsible jerks, including some Communist Party members, jumped on the truck and began giving the milk out to all the women at half price. And did you expect me to run downstairs and take it at that price? Half stolen milk! Would you have done it? And then drunk it?

GIOVANNI. Oh, no, not on your life.

ANTONIA. Good: then don't drink it!

GIOVANNI. But isn't there anything else?

ANTONIA. Yes, I could make you some soup ...

GIOVANNI. Out of what?

ANTONIA. Birdseed for canaries.

GIOVANNI. Birdseed for canaries?

ANTONIA. Yes, it's delicious. It's good for diabetes!

GIOVANNI. But I don't have diabetes!

ANTONIA. Well, I can't help that. Besides, it's half the price of rice. And anyway, there wasn't any long grain rice left.

GIOVANNI. Oh, no, that's too much: first you make out I'm a dog, then a cat, now a canary—

ANTONIA. Oh, quit your bellyaching. Michela, who lives across the hall here, says she makes it every day for her husband, and she swears it's great.

GIOVANNI. For her husband. Yeah, I noticed that he's growing feathers.

ANTONIA. The entire secret is in the stock. Look, I got some rabbit heads too.

GIOVANNI. Rabbit heads?

ANTONIA. Sure. You certainly are ignorant! Birdseed soup is made with rabbit heads—only the heads: frozen! You're not going to tell me you're against frozen food, now?

GIOVANNI. All right, all right . . . I get it . . . So long!

ANTONIA. Where are you going?

GIOVANNI. Where do you think? Out, to some cafe.

ANTONIA. And what about money?

GIOVANNI. Give me some cash.

ANTONIA. What cash?

GIOVANNI. What do you mean, what cash? You're not going to tell me you're broke already!

ANTONIA. No, but did you forget that tomorrow we have to pay the gas and electricity bill, and the rent? Or do you want them to send us an eviction notice and cut off the light and gas!?

GIOVANNI. Of course not.

ANTONIA. Well then, you can forget about the cafe. But don't worry, I'll get you something. (*She puts on her coat.*)

GIOVANNI. Where are you going?

ANTONIA. Over to Margherita's. She went shopping today; she'll lend me some stuff. Don't worry, I'll be back in a minute. In the meantime, read your paper . . . or else go over there and watch TV, I'm sure that the prime minister will be on the screen talking about the economic recession, which is serious but not desperate, saying how we all have to stick together, rich and poor ... Tighten our belts, have patience, understanding, faith in the government and in "Let's Make a Deal." So, while you're having faith in the government and in "Let's Make a Deal," I'll be right back.

GIOVANNI. OK, but without rabbit heads, please.

ANTONIA. Don't worry, this time I'll bring you the paws! (*exits*)

GIOVANNI. Okay, be a smart ass, go ahead ... when I'm so hungry I could even eat ... (*He looks, and reads:*) a tidbit for your little doggie and kitty friends! (*He has picked up a jar and is turning it around in his hands.*) How do you open it? Oh, great; as usual she forgot to get a key. Wait a minute, it's got a screw top. For dogs and cats they make screw top jars!? (*opens the jar*) Here goes! (*sniffs it*) Well, it doesn't smell bad ... it's like pickled marmalade with a base of chopped kidneys, seasoned with cod liver oil. Boy, dogs and cats must really be retarded to eat this crap. Well, I'm going to taste it. But with a few drops of lemon juice to guard against cholera ... (*From outside comes the whine of a police siren, screams of men and women, and military commands.*) What's this racket? (*He glances out the imaginary window and gestures to someone on the other side, in the facing apartment block.*) Aldo, hey, Aldo! What's going on? Yeah, I can see it's the police, but what do they want? Wow, look at all those police vans! What? Something about the supermarket? ... What supermarket? What, here too: The one in this neighborhood? But when ... Today? ... But who ... Everybody? What do you mean, everybody. A thousand women. No, my wife wasn't there, you can be sure about that. She's so much against these ripoffs that she bought me rabbit heads instead . . . yeah, frozen! Besides, today she didn't even leave the house. She had to unwind a girlfriend's belly. No, unravel the bandages, bust it open . . . because her husband, Luigi, doesn't want her to get pregnant, and she obeyed the Pope and so the pill didn't work and she puffed up so much in one week . . . you wouldn't believe it. . . !! What d'you mean, you don't understand? (*He looks down into the street; orders and cries are heard.*) Wow, they're searching everywhere! Are they really trying to go house by house? Well, if they come here to my place, I'll show them! Because this is a clear provocation! A spit in the face. A frame-up. Sure, so they can blame things on us, "those lazy, good-for-nothing thieves, the workers!"

(*a knock at the door*)

VOICE FROM OUTSIDE. Permesso!

GIOVANNI. Who is it?

VOICE. Polizia! Open up!

GIOVANNI. Police? (*opens the door*) What do you want with me?

POLICE SERGEANT. Search. Here's the warrant. Search in the whole block.

GIOVANNI. Why, what are you looking for?

POLICE SERGEANT. (*relaxed, and tired*) Look, you didn't just fall out of the clouds. You know yourself, everybody knows that the supermarket here was looted today. We're looking for the stolen goods, or if you prefer, the merchandise obtained at a five-finger discount.

GIOVANNI. And you're coming to look here, in my house? Meaning I'm a crook, a thug, a bum!

POLICE SERGEANT. Look, take it any way you like. It's

got nothing to do with me. I've got my orders and I have to carry them out.

GIOVANNI. Go right ahead and carry them out . . . but I warn you, this is a provocation. In fact, it's worse: it's a kick in the ass! You come here to fuck around with us, besides starving us to death. Look what I have to eat here: mixed dog and cat rations. (*holds the can out to the officer*)

POLICE SERGEANT. What?

GIOVANNI. Look, look. Smell this crap! And you know why? Because everything costs an arm and a leg! And I don't mean a chicken leg: look here, frozen rabbit heads! (*sticks the package of frozen rabbit heads under the officer's nose*) We can't afford decent stuff—we can't even find it, because it disappears: they hoard it!

SERGEANT. You mean you really eat this stuff?

GIOVANNI. I have no choice . . . anyway, it's not bad, you know! Would you like to try some? Come on, don't stand on ceremony . . . a squeeze of lemon and it goes down like cat shit. Taste it! It's good for sciatica.

SERGEANT. No thanks. I never throw up before meals.

GIOVANNI. Maybe you'd like me to fix you a nice bird-seed soup?

SERGEANT. Birdseed soup? Are you fucking around with me now?

GIOVANNI. I wouldn't dream of it, here it is. It's half the cost of rice . . . eat this and you'll start singing like a canary—you know, tweet, tweet, tweet!

SERGEANT. Boy, you sure are in bad shape! But for that matter it's the same for us, on our wages, it's no joke, my wife has to scrimp and scrape too—even with me getting my meals at the station. Look, I really do understand. And . . . I shouldn't say this, but I also understand all these women in the neighborhood who forced the stores to sell out today. They are right. Personally, I sympathize with them entirely: expropriation is the only defense against robbery!

GIOVANNI. Huh? What? You think they're right?

SERGEANT. Well, sure, things can't go on like this. You may not believe it, but it makes me sick to come around here playing the cop ... going through this lousy search. And who am I doing it for, anyway? — a bunch of dirty speculators who grab stuff, rip it off — they're the ones that are doing the stealing!

GIOVANNI. Excuse me, sergeant ... that's right, isn't it, you are a sergeant?

SERGEANT. Yes, I'm a sergeant.

GIOVANNI. Good ... is that a proper way to talk? A policeman, for crying out loud! You know you're talking like an extremist?

SERGEANT. Extremist, nothing, I'm a person who uses his head. And gets pissed off, too — you have to stop considering ordinary policemen a bunch of morons who just jump whenever they hear a whistle: Attention! At your orders! Quick, bark, bite — like guard dogs! And God help you if you try to talk, discuss things ... never express your own opinions ... Shut up! Lie down and be good!

VOICE FROM OUTSIDE. Sergeant! Now where did he go? Sergeant!

SERGEANT. (*goes to door, yells:*) Here I am, on the second floor ... I'm doing a house search. You go on upstairs, to the other floors. (*returns to discussion*)

GIOVANNI. All right, OK ... I guess I'll go along with what the Party Secretary Belinguer says, that you're workers too, "sons of the people," ... but —

SERGEANT. Sons of the people, my ass — we're guard dogs. They turn us into lackeys of the people in power, the boss's thugs . . . We're supposed to enforce respect for their laws, and dirty tricks.

GIOVANNI. Wait a moment: if that's how you think, why did you choose this job?

SERGEANT. Who chose what? Just like you chose to eat this crap for dogs and cats, rabbit heads, and that other garbage for canaries?

GIOVANNI. No, that's all there was!

SERGEANT. There you are! That's all there was for me too . . . take it or drop dead. I happen to be a college graduate.

A MALE VOICE FROM OUTSIDE. Sergeant, we've finished here . . . What should we do now, go on ahead?

SERGEANT. (*goes to door, yells:*) Of course, don't just stand there giving me a pain in the ass! (*returns to discussion*) As I was saying, I'm a college graduate. My father went without for years so that I could go to school . . . And in the end what did I find? A city job sweeping streets, waiting on tables in Switzerland, or the police force! I had to take this job! "Join the police force and learn the ways of the world." Boy, some ways! Some world! A world of bastards, swindlers, and suckers!

GIOVANNI. Yeah, but not everybody thinks that way. Some guys get along fine in the police force.

SERGEANT. Oh, sure, the ones snowed by propaganda: "A sense of honor and sacrifice." To feel they're somebody these guys have to repress other people, give orders, and bust a few heads; they're the retarded sons of this nation of sheep!

GIOVANNI. (*to audience*) It's unbelievable . . . if I hadn't heard it with my own two ears, I'd never believe it. (*to Sergeant*) But in the end we need the police . . . don't we? Maybe a little more democratic, but we need them. If not, we'd have chaos! Just because it comes into your head that something's right doesn't mean you can act on it . . . (*Without noticing it, he's shaking the rabbit heads.*) . . . like going shopping and paying whatever you think is right. You've got to obey the law!

SERGEANT. And what if the law's rotten, just a cover for grand larceny?

GIOVANNI. Well, then there's a parliament, there are the parties . . . democratic methods of struggle . . . and laws can be reformed—

SERGEANT. What d'you mean, reforms? What reforms, where? A con, that's what they are. For twenty years they've been promising us reforms . . . and the only ones that have passed are those that pull the grafters up by *our* bootstraps: reforms that raise the price of gasoline, telephone, electricity . . . what about the one that handed out forty billion lire to the political parties for their election campaigns. First they steal in business, and then as punishment we let these fucking thieves in the government, where they decide to finance themselves . . . another ripoff, this time legalized! And the Communist Party's in it too!

GIOVANNI. Well, you're right about that—I didn't like that pig shit either.

SERGEANT. Believe me, the only serious reforms will be made by the people, in their own name, when they really start thinking. Because as long as the people "delegate . . . ," "put their trust . . . ," "have patience, a sense of responsibility, understanding, self-control, self-discipline" and on and on like this . . . *nothing changes!* And now, please excuse me, I have to go and do my job.

GIOVANNI. There, you see! First you act the Maoist subversive, and then, when it comes down to it, you put on your cap, and go back to being a cop.

SERGEANT. You're right, I'm just one of those guys who's all talk. I let off steam and that's that. Obviously, I don't have enough courage and consciousness. For now, I'm just a shit-slinger.

GIOVANNI. Right! All talk ... The poor college graduate who has to be a cop because he's got no other choice! D'you expect me to cry over your problems? "But I can't really emigrate, you know, I'm a college graduate." In fact, you should have emigrated too, or else swept streets, like other guys in your home town ...*They've* made a man's choice—because they've got dignity. Got it? It's a matter of dignity! But guys like you are always ready with an excuse so they never risk anything. Yeah, and tomorrow you'll be there in front of the factory as usual ready to beat me up when there's a strike.

SERGEANT. Correct; you're right again. But you never know ... maybe one of these days you'll hear that some cops have refused to go do the dirty work for the bosses ... that they've even gone over to the other side!

GIOVANNI. Oh, I'll wait for the day. But first I expect to see the Pope dressed as an Indian!

SERGEANT. Look, the world's changing. It's changing a lot. So long and have a nice meal!

GIOVANNI. So now you're taking off like that, without even doing a little search? Now I'm offended! Take a little peek, just for fun ... under the bed, in the closet ... for instance.

SERGEANT. What for? Just to find a package of pig food and a can of meal for home-grown trout? Thanks, but there's no need. So long, and buon appetite! (*exits*)

GIOVANNI. Altre tanto! Boy, the number of weirdos you run into! A cop who's a wild red subversive! I've met fascists, thugs, and bullies, and now. So here's where the political extremists wind up ... in the police force ... and he stands there criticizing the Communist Party as not revolutionary enough! If only they knew it. Some "sons of the people." Ah, now I get it ... he's a provocateur. The wise guy comes here to try and put words into my mouth: "We have to loot the supermarkets ... the police should revolt" ... and if I'd fallen for it like an asshole and agreed with him, he'd have pounced on me: "hands up ... Red Brigades ... you're under arrest ... where've you hidden Moro." ... Oh, yeah! You found the fish who'd bite all right. (*Absent-mindedly he grabs the package of birdseed.*) ... the fish who'd swallow the bait and the hook too? ... No. Here the fish only eats canary food!

(*ANTONIA enters with MARGHERITA, the latter's belly still swollen up and covered with her overcoat. MARGHERITA peeks in the doorway, then quickly backs off.*)

ANTONIA. Have they been here too?

GIOVANNI. Who?

ANTONIA. Don't you know what's going on? ... That they're searching house by house?

GIOVANNI. Sure I know it.

ANTONIA. They even arrested the Mambettis and the Fosanis ... They found stuff in lots of apartments and confiscated everything.

GIOVANNI. It serves them right, that'll teach 'em to act so smart.

ANTONIA. But they even took stuff that was fully paid for.

GIOVANNI. Sure, it's always the same; when a few creeps rip stuff off, people who don't have anything to do with it get into trouble — For instance, they came here and . . .

ANTONIA. They came? Here?

GIOVANNI. Sure.

ANTONIA. What did they find?

GIOVANNI. Why? What should they have found?

ANTONIA. No, I mean . . . you never know . . . sometimes you think you don't have anything in the house, and then . . .

GIOVANNI. And then?

ANTONIA. And then?

GIOVANNI. And then?

ANTONIA. And then they plant the stuff there themselves, to frame you . . . It wouldn't be the first time. For instance, they searched at Rosa's son's place, and just like that, pop! they snuck in a pistol under the pillow and a pack of leaflets under the bed.

GIOVANNI. Ma che brava! You think they'd come here to put packages of pasta and sugar under the bed?

ANTONIA. Well, maybe not under the bed, no . . . You know what I mean . . .

GIOVANNI. Yeah, I know . . . but maybe you're right . . . You never know . . . I'll have a look.

ANTONIA. No!

GIOVANNI. What d'you mean, no?

ANTONIA. Well, I mean . . . you'll put your dirty hands all over the pillow . . . I'll take a look myself . . . You let in Margherita.

GIOVANNI. Margherita? Where is she?

MARGHERITA. (*loud cry*) Ahhh!

GIOVANNI. Where?

MARGHERITA. Here!

ANTONIA. There, outside the door. (*She pretends to look under the bed.*) No, nothing here.

GIOVANNI. But why'd you leave her standing out there? Oh, good god, Margherita, what are you doing there? Come in, come in. (*MARGHERITA enters, sobbing.*) What happened to her?

ANTONIA. Ah, she was all alone in her apartment, poor kid . . . and when she saw all those cops charging in, she got scared. Imagine, there was a lieutenant who wanted to feel her belly.

MARGHERITA. (*loud cry*)

GIOVANNI. Bastard! Why?

ANTONIA. Because he got the idea that instead of a baby up there, she had packages of pasta and other stuff.

GIOVANNI. What a dirty sonofabitch!

ANTONIA. You said it . . . C'mere, Margherita, sit down on the bed. So I told her to come to our place. Did I do the right thing?

GIOVANNI. Sure you did the right thing. But take off your coat, Margherita.

MARGHERITA. No thanks.

GIOVANNI. Come on, don't be so formal. Take it off.

ANTONIA. Ah, let her be. She said she'd rather keep it on. Maybe she's cold.

GIOVANNI. But it's hot in here.

ANTONIA. You find it hot, but she finds it cold. Maybe she even has a fever!

GIOVANNI. A fever? Is she sick?

ANTONIA. Sure; she's having labor pains!

MARGHERITA. (*two loud cries*)

GIOVANNI. Already?

ANTONIA. Whaddya mean, already? What do you know about it? Half an hour ago you didn't even know she was pregnant, and now you're amazed that she's having labor pains!

GIOVANNI. Well, it seems to me ... I dunno ... It seems to me a little premature!

ANTONIA. There he goes again! What do you know about it, if it's premature or not? You think you know more about it than she does? She's having the pains! Come on, get undressed ... undress and get under the covers. And you: do me a favor: turn around.

GIOVANNI. Sure, sure, I'll turn around. (*does it*)

ANTONIA. Come on! Don't tremble like that ... don't cry ... it's all over now.

GIOVANNI. But if she's having labor pains, we'd better call a doctor. Or maybe even an ambulance.

ANTONIA. Aren't you bright: an ambulance! And then we'll go on a nice wild goose chase to every hospital in town ... back and forth ... because we'll never find an empty bed! Oh boy, what a great way for the baby to be born! Don't you know that with the chaos they've got in the hospitals, people like us on the health plan, have to reserve a bed at least a month in advance?

GIOVANNI. So how come she didn't preregister?

ANTONIA. Oh, yeah, sure, why didn't she preregister: Us women always have to take care of everything: we have to do the running around, we have the kids, we make the reservations; And why didn't her husband do it?

GIOVANNI. But how could he, if he didn't know about it?

ANTONIA. That's a great excuse: he didn't know ... You men are always like that—take the easy way out. You hand us the paycheck and then you say, "You take care of it; you work it out!" You make love—because you've got a sacred right—you get us pregnant, and then it's, "you work it out. Take the pill." And who gives a damn if the poor wife, who's a devout Catholic, every night dreams of the Pope saying to her: "you're committing a sin; you must procreate!"

GIOVANNI. So the Pope comes to mess you up even in your dreams, and even on television saying, "love one anotherski, we're all Gold's childrenski, rich and poor—especially the rich!' But what I mean, or rather what I want to know, is: when did Margherita get pregnant?

ANTONIA. What's it to you? And what's all this putting down the Popeski?

GIOVANNI. No, I mean—if they haven't even been married five months?

ANTONIA. So, they couldn't have started having sex earlier? Or are you a goddamn moralist, too, worse than the Pope?

GIOVANNI. No, but her husband, Luigi, told me that they made love for the first time only after they were married!

MARGHERITA. Did my Luigi tell you all that?

ANTONIA. But that's incredible—going around telling intimate things like that to anyone who comes along!

GIOVANNI. I'm not anyone who comes along! I'm his friend! His best friend! And he always tells me everything, asks me for advice ... because I'm older and more experienced.

ANTONIA. Oh, get that: more experienced! (*another knock at the door*) Who is it?

VOICE FROM OUTSIDE. Police, open up!

GIOVANNI. Again?

MARGHERITA. Omigod!

GIOVANNI. (*opening the door*) Buono serra ... is it you again? (*In fact, we see the same actor who played*

the role of the POLICE SERGEANT, but now he is
wearing the insignia of a lieutenant in the Carabinieri,
and has a mustache.)

LIEUTENANT. What do you mean, you again?

GIOVANNI. Oh, sorry, I thought you were the one who
was here before.

LIEUTENANT. Which one was here before?

GIOVANNI. A police sergeant.

LIEUTENANT. Well, I happen to be a lieutenant in the
Carabinieri.

GIOVANNI. I can see that, besides, you have a
mustache. Okay, what is it you want?

LIEUTENANT. We have to make a search.

GIOVANNI. But your fellow-officers in the police
department already just made one.

LIEUTENANT. That doesn't matter! We'll do it over
again.

GIOVANNI. Ah, you don't trust them, so you came
back to make sure we haven't pulled any fast ones! Then
maybe the Treasury Department will come to check up
on you; then they'll send in the secret police and finally,
the Marines.

LIEUTENANT. Stop wisecracking—get over there and
let us do our job.

ANTONIA. Of course, everybody has to get on with his
job! We break our backs in the factory for eight hours a
day at the looms ... you put in eight hours on the
assembly line, like a bunch of animals ... and they
work to make sure we toe the line—that we pay the price
the bosses ask for their merchandise! (*The Carabinieri*
open the cupboard and closet.) Do you ever happen by
any chance to check on whether the bosses are following
their contracts and not killing us with piece-work or

dumping us on unemployment? Check to make sure they're following the health and safety regulations?

(*The LIEUTENANT continues his search undisturbed.*)

GIOVANNI. No, you shouldn't talk like that, because it disgusts them too! Isn't that right, Lieutenant, that it makes you sick to carry out these searches and arrests for the bosses? You tell my wife how you policemen are fed up to here with taking orders every time a whistle blows—Attention! Jump up! Bark! Bite! like guard dogs—and god help you if you argue. Lie down, heel.

LIEUTENANT. Say that again. What's this about guard dogs?

GIOVANNI. Yes, I said you aren't sons of the people, like the communists say . . . you're servants of the ruling class—the boss's thugs!

LIEUTENANT. Handcuffs! (*removes cuffs from self*)

GIOVANNI. Handcuffs? Why, what for?

LIEUTENANT. For offense and insult to a public officer.

GIOVANNI. What d'you mean, insulting? I'm not the one who said those things—it was your fellow officer, a little while ago, he was the one who said you feel like lackeys of the ruling class!

LIEUTENANT. You, who? Us carabinieri?

GIOVANNI. No, he said you, meaning them—the ones in the Police Department.

LIEUTENANT. Oh, well, if those guys in the police force feel like lackeys, that's their problem. But watch what you say!

GIOVANNI. Sure, sure, I'll watch it. Boy, are these separate institutions ever separate!

(*The Carabinieri goes on with his search, now approaching the bed.*)

ANTONIA. (*to MARGHERITA*) Start moaning! Come on, cry.

MARGHERITA. Aiaooaoo!

ANTONIA. Louder!

MARGHERITA. (*moaning as if in extreme pain*) Ahiouua! Aiaaooioo!

LIEUTENANT. What's going on? What's the matter with her?

ANTONIA. She's having labor pains, poor kid!

GIOVANNI. Premature delivery, five months at the most.

ANTONIA. She got into a state a little while ago ... because some cops tried to feel her stomach, poor kid!

LIEUTENANT. Feel her stomach?

GIOVANNI. Sure, to see if, instead of a baby, she maybe had a couple of packages of rice or pasta stuffed up there. Go on, why don't you help yourself. Sure, she's just a poor factory worker, you won't get into any trouble ... you're allowed. Now if you took liberties with Princess Grace or poked your finger up Pirelli's wife you'd get thrown straight out of the force. But there's no risk here — one poke to a customer.

LIEUTENANT. Listen, stop that! You're provoking us!

ANTONIA. Yeah, you're overdoing it — cut it out!

MARGHERITA. (*very loud*) Aiuaaiiiaaiiiii! Auhiaaa!

ANTONIA. Don't you overdo it too.

LIEUTENANT. But did you call an ambulance?

ANTONIA. An ambulance?

LIEUTENANT. Well, you can't leave this poor woman here to maybe die. And if it's premature like you say, she could lose the baby.

GIOVANNI. He's right. You see, you see how

understanding the Lieutenant is? I told you before you should call an ambulance.

ANTONIA. And I told you before that without a reservation they won't accept her. They'll send her chasing from one hospital to another all over town. That way she'll croak in the ambulance! (*The howling of a siren is heard outside.*)

LIEUTENANT. (*going over and looking out the window*) There, an ambulance is coming to pick up that other woman who got sick on the next floor down. Come on, give me a hand. Let's load her on too.

ANTONIA. (*resisting*) No, for heaven's sake . . . don't go to any trouble.

MARGHERITA. No, I don't want to go to the hospital!

ANTONIA. You see, she doesn't want to.

MARGHERITA. I want my husband, my husband . . . Ahio! Ahiuuaoo!

ANTONIA. You hear, she wants her husband . . . But he can't be here because he's on the night shift. I'm sorry, but without her husband's consent, we can't take this responsibility.

GIOVANNI. Oh, no, we can't take it.

LIEUTENANT. You won't take it, eh? But you'd take the responsibility for letting her drop dead here?

ANTONIA. Instead of the hospital?

LIEUTENANT. At the hospital they could save her, and maybe the baby, too!

GIOVANNI. But it's premature, I told you!

MARGHERITA. Yes, yes, I'm premature . . .

ANTONIA. And with the ambulance jolting she'll give birth! And how can a five-months' old baby survive?

LIEUTENANT. Obviously you have no idea of modern medical progress. Didn't you ever read about test-tube babies?

ANTONIA. Yes, I did, but what do test-tubes have to

do with it? And you can't put a five-month baby in an oxygen tent!

GIOVANNI. That's right, such a teeny thing, under a tent — doing what, anyway? Camping out?

LIEUTENANT. It's clear that you're starved for information.

ANTONIA and GIOVANNI. Oh yes, we're starved, all right!

LIEUTENANT. Where have you been hiding out? Haven't you ever seen the equipment they've got now, right here in Milan, at the gynecology clinic? I was on duty in there five months ago, and I saw they're even doing transplants.

MARGHERITA, ANTONIA, and GIOVANNI. A transplant of what?

LIEUTENANT. A premature baby transplant. (*He demonstrates.*) They took a four-and-a-half month baby out of the womb of a woman who couldn't carry him, and they fixed him in another woman's womb.

GIOVANNI. Right inside her?

LIEUTENANT. Just like that. Caesarian: they transplanted it with the placenta and everything . . . sewed her up, and four months later — just last month, in fact, out came the baby again, as fine and healthy as a fish.

GIOVANNI. A fish?

LIEUTENANT. Yep!

GIOVANNI. Must be a trick.

ANTONIA. Trick, nothing, I read about it too. Sure it's incredible — a baby born twice . . . a kid with two mothers!

MARGHERITA. No, no, I don't want to! Ahiouu!

ANTONIA. She's right, poor kid . . . hell, I'd never let another woman give birth to my child either!

MARGHERITA. I don't want to, I don't want to! I won't give my consent!

ANTONIA. There, you hear. She won't give her consent ... so we can't take her away from here.

LIEUTENANT. Well then, I'll give my consent; I'll take the responsibility! I don't want trouble for neglecting to provide necessary aid!

ANTONIA. But that's just plain force and violence: first they poke all over the house, then they handcuff us ... now they want to shove us into an ambulance. You won't let us live, OK, but at least let us die where we choose!

LIEUTENANT. No, you can't die where you choose.

GIOVANNI. Sure, we have to die where the law decides!

LIEUTENANT. And you watch it with the snide remarks. I already warned you—

GIOVANNI. So who's making snide remarks?

ANTONIA. Take it from me, Giovanni, this isn't the right moment. Come on, let's carry her down.

LIEUTENANT. Should I call for the stretcher?

ANTONIA. No, no, she can come by herself. You can walk, can't you? Now we'll just help her up ...

MARGHERITA. Yes, yes—oh, no, no—it's slipping out!

ANTONIA. Omigod! Do you mind going out for a minute? My friend is kind of undressed, and I have to help her get her clothes back on.

LIEUTENANT. Right, let's go. (*All the men exit.*)

ANTONIA. C'mon, hurry, lift up these bags. Dammit, that lousy ambulance was all we needed!

MARGHERITA. I knew it would end badly! And what'll happen at the hospital when they find out I'm pregnant with pasta, rice and canned goods?

ANTONIA. Nothing will happen, because we won't get to the hospital.

MARGHERITA. Sure, because we'll get arrested first!

ANTONIA. Just cut out the whining: once we're inside

the ambulance, we'll tell the medical assistants what's going on ... They're good people, those guys, they're on our side ... they'll help us out for sure.

MARGHERITA. What if they're not on our side? And they report us?

ANTONIA. Cut it out, they won't report us!

MARGHERITA. It's slipping down; I'm losing another bag!

ANTONIA. Hold onto it! Good grief, what a pain in the ass!

MARGHERITA. No, don't push ... Dammit, something just broke open ... a packet of olives in juice! Yech!

(*At this moment GIOVANNI appears, followed by the LIEUTENANT.*)

GIOVANNI. What's going on now?

MARGHERITA. It's coming out; it's all coming out!

GIOVANNI. The baby's coming out! The baby's coming out! Quick, Lieutenant, help me carry her!

LIEUTENANT. Let me do that!

ANTONIA. There we are ... good ... keep her horizontal.

LIEUTENANT. What's this wet spot?

ANTONIA. Oh, she must be losing water.

GIOVANNI. Quick; if we don't hurry, she'll be having the baby in here!

ANTONIA. Cool down, cool down, take it easy!

MARGHERITA. It's coming, it's coming out!

ANTONIA. (*sottovoce to MARGHERITA*) I know it's coming out! (*to others*) Hold on, let's wrap her up in this blanket. Take it easy, Lieutenant!

GIOVANNI. Wait a minute, I'll get my jacket and come too.

ANTONIA. No, stay at home! You take a cloth and wipe up the floor where it's all wet. This is women's business. (*exit, all except GIOVANNI*)

GIOVANNI. (*grabs the rag and goes to wipe up the floor*) Yeah, sure ... I'll take a rag and wipe ... that's men's business. What a mess! Luigi'll have a surprise when he comes off the shift tomorrow ... and finds himself a father all at one stroke ... He'll *have* a stroke! And when he finds out his baby has been transplanted into another woman, he'll have another stroke ... and that'll finish him off! I'd better speak to him first, prepare him gradually, kind of come in through the back door! I know! I'll begin by talking about the Pope ... "My brothers in Christ!" (*He's down on all fours, wiping the floor with the rag.*) Wow, look at all that water! What a weird odor, it smells like vinegar ... yes, like olive juice, sure! I never knew that ... that before we're born, we spend nine months in olive juice! Oh, look ... what's this? An olive? We sit in juice with olives? I can't believe it! That's crazy! The olive's got nothing to do with it. (*Once again the howl of a siren is heard; GIOVANNI gets up and returns to the window.*) Well, they're driving off. Let's hope everything comes out alright ... But where'd this olive come from? And look, another one: two olives? If they weren't of such uncertain origin ... I'd eat them, I'm so hungry! I'm almost tempted to make a soup with birdseed for real. Maybe it's even good. The water's on the stove already ... I'll just put in a couple of bouillon cubes ... and a head of garlic ... (*opens the refrigerator*) I knew it! No bouillon cubes, and not a single head of garlic ... I guess I have put in a rabbit head instead! I feel like the witch in Snow White fixing up the poison potion. Then you'll see, I eat the soup and bam! I turn into a frog!

(*Without thinking he grabs the starter.*) Hey, what's my portable starter doing here? How many times do I have to tell that idiot Antonia that she shouldn't use it to light the stove, it's dangerous! And besides, it runs down the batteries.

(*LUIGI looks in from the door.*)

LUIGI. Can I come in? Anybody home?

GIOVANNI. Ciao, Luigi! Aren't you on the night shift? What are you doing here at this hour?

LUIGI. Something happened on the way to the factory . . . I'll explain later. Right now, do you know where my wife is? I might as well throw my keys away. (*He throws them onto the cupboard.*) I was just home, and everything's wide open, but nobody's there.

GIOVANNI. Right; your wife was here ten minutes ago, and left with Antonia.

LUIGI. Where'd they go? And what for?

GIOVANNI. Well, you know; "women's business."

LUIGI. What do you mean, "women's business"?

GIOVANNI. Hey, cool down! What's got into you? When I say "women's business," I mean things that aren't men's business.

LUIGI. But why shouldn't it be any of my business? It *is* my business!

GIOVANNI. Oh, sure, it's your business. Well then, how come you didn't make it your business to reserve a bed a month ago, like everybody else does?

LUIGI. A bed? A bed for what?

GIOVANNI. Oh, yeah, that's women's business, isn't it! The usual song and dance! We shove our paycheck at 'em and then tell 'em: "You work it out!" We have sex, and we tell 'em: "Take the pill!" We get 'em pregnant and, "It's your problem!" They have the baby, and they're the ones that have to take it to nursery school, pick it up . . .

LUIGI. What the hell are you talking about?

GIOVANNI. I'm talking about that they're right; we really are irresponsible jerks! We're exploiters, the same as the bosses!

LUIGI. But what's all this got to do with the fact that Margherita leaves the apartment door wide open and disappears just like that, without even leaving me a note?

GIOVANNI. Why should she leave you a note? Aren't you supposed to be at the plant on the night shift? So how come you're already back?

LUIGI. Well, the train was held up.

GIOVANNI. Who held it up?

LUIGI. All of us workers, because those sons-a-bitches raised the price of our commuter pass thirty percent!

GIOVANNI. And for that you held up the train?

LUIGI. Sure, we pulled the emergency cord, and everybody jumped down on the tracks! We blocked the whole line. Even the Rome express and the International for Paris! You should have seen how pissed off the first-class passengers were!

GIOVANNI. Ah, a great party? Very impressive! Sorry, but in my book only brainless troublemakers would pull a stunt like that. Dumb, shithead tricks, playing into the hands of the reactionaries!

LUIGI. Yeah, you're right, they're dumb shithead tricks! I even told them, "There is no point in making this stink over raising the price; we shouldn't be paying for the pass in the first place!"

GIOVANNI. Oh, bravo . . . you're really crazy! Not pay for the pass!

LUIGI. Sure, the company ought to pay for our transportation! And they ought to pay us for the time we spend in the train too! Portal to portal pay. Because all that travelling isn't for sightseeing; we get up two hours early and come home two hours late . . . all for the company.

GIOVANNI. Are you serious? Who've you been talking to? Those wild men on the far left, I bet . . . they're all police agents and provacateurs!

LUIGI. Don't talk horseshit, provocateurs! Is Tonino a provocateur?

GIOVANNI. Tonino that works the presses?

LUIGI. Yeah, him. And Marco, and the three Calabrians from my home town?

GIOVANNI. So, you've been listening to those southern Italians? Those Arab hijackers!

LUIGI. No, I thought it all on my own. It's obvious that things can't go on like this; we gotta move without waiting for the good wishes of the government, or the intervention of the unions or a good word from the party. We gotta stop waiting for permission to do everything even taking a piss. "Wait," "have faith," "sense of responsibility," "be understanding." No, we've got to get things moving ourselves.

GIOVANNI. Tell me: have you been talking to that police sergeant without a mustache who's the spitting image of the Carabinieri lieutenant with a mustache?

LUIGI. Who?

GIOVANNI. Yeah, that cop, the maoist provocateur who says we gotta go shoplifting in the supermarkets; that guy makes the same brainless hothead speeches you do!

LUIGI. Never heard of him. (*He tastes the contents of the open jar.*) Hm, not bad, this stuff. What is it?

GIOVANNI. Huh? You ate the stuff in that jar?

LUIGI. Sure, it's not bad. Sorry, but I was hungry.

GIOVANNI. Without lemon?

LUIGI. Yes, why, do you eat it with lemon?

GIOVANNI. Bah, I don't know. Sure it's good?

LUIGI. Wonderful.

GIOVANNI. Let me taste ... Well, I thought it'd be worse; it's almost better than than concentrate they use for carp fishing. Would you mind opening this other jar too?

LUIGI. Sure, but what is it?

GIOVANNI. It's a kind of paté for rich dogs and cats.

LUIGI. Paté for dogs and cats? Are you nuts?

GIOVANNI. No, I'm an eccentric ... a gourmet? Try this. (*He brings LUIGI a bowl of soup.*) Taste it, taste it!

LUIGI. Huh, not bad. What is it?

GIOVANNI. Oh, a speciality of mine: canary seed in a broth of frozen rabbit heads?

LUIGI. Canary seed and rabbit heads?

GIOVANNI. Sure, it's a Chinese dish; they call it Mush a la Deng Xiaping ... Revisionist cooking.

LUIGI. But the birdseed's a bit raw ...

GIOVANNI. What d'you mean? It's birdseed pilaf, it's always served a bit crisp ... Yes, crispy birdseed and crappy rabbit heads. That's the way they started the cultural counterrevolution in China! By the way, who ate the olive that was sitting here?

LUIGI. I did. Why, wasn't I supposed to?

GIOVANNI. No, you were not supposed to! It was your wife's olive! Man, you'll even steal your newborn baby's food!

LUIGI. What? My wife's olive ... my newborn baby?

GIOVANNI. Ah, yes, because when you're born, you

see, the juice comes out . . . Well, forget it, I'd better go slowly . . . start with the Pope . . . Now, His Eminence John Paul . . .

LUIGI. Look, Giovanni, are you feeling OK? What kind of talk is this?

GIOVANNI. Talk? Oh yeah; you're the one who knows the right way to talk. The boss should pay for our ticket because we travel for him . . . and for the time we spend on the train too . . . Next you'll be saying he should pay us for the time we sleep, because we're resting up for his sake, so we can be nice and fresh for work the next day; and he should even pay for our movies and our TV set because that junk helps us unwind our nerves after working on the line. And he ought to pay our wives, too, every time they have sex with us because it makes us feel better so we produce more!

LUIGI. Ecco Bravo! And isn't it true that our wives really slave for the boss without pay? And when the boss makes us mad, we take it out on them? All that—what do you call it—alienation we get from the factory. We come back home and quarrel like dogs in a compound. (*imitating two puppet voices:*)

M: Where's the milk?
F: There is no milk.
M: Why no milk?
F: There is no money.
M: What you mean, no money!
M & F: (*Both fight.*)
Husband and wife!

GIOVANNI. Don't exaggerate now. Life isn't all that shitty, come on. Things are better than they used to be! Almost everybody has a house now, even if it's lousy. Some of us even have a car, and everybody has a refrigerator, and a TV set . . .

LUIGI. What do I care about a refrigerator, a car, or a TV set, when the work I do makes me want to puke? Jesus Christ! Our job is like a trained monkey act: a weld, a rap with the hammer, a shot with the drill, a weld, a rap, one part gone, another in place ... a weld and (*GIOVANNI begins to pick up the motion of the assembly-line work; gradually he speaks with LUIGI, then he adds sounds, building:*) ... a rap ... the line speeds up ... a weld ...

GIOVANNI with LUIGI. ... rap ... a shot with the drill ... one part gone, another in place ... A weld ...

GIOVANNI. (*breaking the rhythm*) Hey, for Chrissake, what are you making me do? You're scrambling my brain, too!

LUIGI. No, it's not me who's scrambling your brain, it's the boss! The same boss that messes you up inside everywhere: at the movies with stories about impossible fucks with little asses all over the place ... women acting like panthers in heat ... talking and moving their mouth and tongue like they're licking an ice cream cone, and I don't know what else. And that's what they call adult movies.

GIOVANNI. Yeah! And what about when you leave the movies? You're taking a nice little relaxing stroll with your wife and you pass those billboards with more tits and ass, advertising ball point pens, toothpaste, cheese spread. There's your wife, walking next to you. You look at her ... she doesn't have her hair washed in Dreck, "soft, manageable, and lustrous," she doesn't wear nail polish with "glowing color," she doesn't wear perfume, "Love me tender!" Her tits are just plain round things ... they don't even bounce. Her behind is only a behind; it's not a "little ass" like the ones in the movies. She has swollen feet and chapped hands; I take

one look at her and get the urge to knock her into the
first ditch I see!

LUIGI. Right! There you are, good! You know what
happens to me? When I have sex with my wife? I don't
make love with her, I make love with Signal toothpaste,
the one with the red stripes ... with Black Velvet
Scotch, "smooth and blonde," and with Aqua Velva!

GIOVANNI. Man, it really makes you sick!

LUIGI. It makes you sick because the bosses have
made it that way. You've been infected all over. They've
poisoned the air we breathe, they've poisoned our rivers,
they've turned the sea into a sewer. They've made
human relations into a cesspool, love into sewage and
people into shit ... even the food you eat!

GIOVANNI. Well, not everything. For instance, this
birdseed soup isn't bad!

LUIGI. Everything's going to pot ... look: factories
closing; layoffs, unemployment ... and the collapse of
that bank where even the Pope had his billions stashed.

GIOVANNI. It serves him right, that old scarecrow going around in a white dress, giving women a pain in the
ass about getting pregnant!

LUIGI. What d'you mean, the Pope's getting pregnant?

GIOVANNI. No, not him ... though he'd probably like
it ... I'm talking about your wife.

LUIGI. What's my wife got to do with the Pope?

GIOVANNI. Oh, you're pretending you don't know?

LUIGI. No, I *don't* know! What's this thing about the
Pope?

GIOVANNI. There you are! Instead of making love
with striped toothpaste and Aqua Velva, if you paid attention to what your wife dreams at night, when his
Eminence John Paul comes in his white robe and starts

saying "Brothers in Christ, I come to tell you that the pill is God's curse ... For Christ's sake, don't take the pill!"

LUIGI. Well, in fact Margherita doesn't take the pill.

GIOVANNI. Ah, so you knew it. Who told you?

LUIGI. Who was supposed to tell me? She doesn't need to take it since she can't have babies anyway, something's wrong inside, can't remember exactly.

GIOVANNI. You're the one who's got something wrong in your head! Your wife is fit as a fiddle, and can have babies! In fact she's got one now!

LUIGI. She has a baby? Since when?

GIOVANNI. Since right now! It's probably already born, five months premature!

LUIGI. Don't give me that crap; five months! She didn't even have a belly!

GIOVANNI. No, she didn't have one because she'd bandaged herself up; then Antonia untied her, and ploof! a belly that looked like nine months ... or maybe even eleven!

LUIGI. Listen, are you fuckin' around with my head?

GIOVANNI. Not me! Fact is, if you really want to know, my wife's gone with her to the hospital in an ambulance, because she was almost about ready to have the baby here.

LUIGI. Have the baby here!

GIOVANNI. She was already losing water ... look, I wiped it up myself.

LUIGI. You wiped up my wife's water?

GIOVANNI. Well, water ... Maybe it would be more accurate to call it "juice" with an olive or two, which actually you've just eaten.

LUIGI. Quit kidding around! Where's my wife?

GIOVANNI. I told you, at the hospital.

LUIGI. Which hospital?

GIOVANNI. Who knows? If you'd preregistered, now we'd know. But this way she may be going from one place to the other, with the baby coming out in the ambulance, poor little bambino, among all the olives!

LUIGI. Stop acting like an asshole! Always making wisecracks, and kidding even about serious things! Tell me what hospital they took her to or I'll smack you in the teeth!

GIOVANNI. Hey, cool it! I told you, I don't know ... Wait a minute, maybe they went to that place, whaddyacallit, the geanological clinic.

LUIGI. The gynecological clinic?

GIOVANNI. Yeah, where they also transplant premature babies.

LUIGI. Transplant babies?

GIOVANNI. Yeah, really. Where have you been? It's obvious you're starved for information about premature birth so I'll just explain. They do it like this: there's this big oxygen tent ... They take the woman with the premature baby, four and a half, maybe five months ... Then they take this woman who's the second mother ... do a Caesarian on her ... put the baby in her belly, sew up the placenta and everything ... and then after four months (*pauses*) ... a fish.

LUIGI. Cut it out about transplants and Caesarians ... just tell me where this goddam gynecological clinic is. You got a phone book?

GIOVANNI. No, I don't. What would I do with it, without a phone? I guess I could read it for fun, just to find out who's in town!

LUIGI. Then let's go downstairs to the bar. They've got a phone there.

GIOVANNI. It just came back to me, the gynecological clinic is in Niguarda!

LUIGI. Niguarda?

GIOVANNI. Yeah, it's at least twenty kilometers from here.

LUIGI. But why'd they go there?

GIOVANNI. I told you; God, what a shithead. It's because that's where they do the transplants; they take another woman, the first volunteer ... Another woman? My wife! Antonia would do it for sure ... She'd be the first volunteer! She's so dumb! Get going! She'll let them do the transplant for sure, and she'll come back home pregnant!

CURTAIN

END OF ACT I

ACT II

LUIGI and GIOVANNO cross apron, on their way to the hospital, singing "Avanti Popolo." Curtain. ANTONIA and MARGHERITA are coming back into the apartment. MARGHERITA is whining, she still has her big belly.

ANTONIA. Hurry up, Margherita, come in. (*calling out*) Giovanni, Giovanni! Not here, he must have gone to work already. What time is it? (*looks at the alarm clock on the cupboard*) Five-thirty. Madonna, what with one thing and another, we've been gone more than four hours. (*goes to glance into the other room*) Yeah, he really has gone. And he didn't even get to bed, poor guy.

MARGHERITA. It's all your fault; why did I listen to you! Now look, we're in shit up to our ears.

ANTONIA. Stop moaning, dammit, you really arc a crybaby! So what happened finally? Everything went as smooth as silk, didn't it? Didn't you see how nice those guys in the ambulance were? We just told them: "Look, the kid here isn't pregnant, just big with loot," and they jumped at the chance to help us. They even congratulated us! "Che brave! You women are terrific! It's great what you did! Those thieving profiteers at the supermarket deserve a good beating!" And you were so worried: you should learn to trust people! (*She looks in the refrigerator.*) Hey, who stole my butter? No, no, here it is. Now I'll make you some soup. Oh, the rice, give me a package of rice. (*MARGHERITA pulls a package of rice out of a bag hidden under her coat. ANTONIA goes to the stove and sees the pan there.*) But what's this stuff? Birdseed? That big deficient Giovanni really made himself some soup with the birdseed and rabbit heads! Do you believe it! You can't even tell him a lie without him swallowing it.

MARGHERITA. Look, if you're making the soup just for me, don't bother, I'm not hungry. My stomach has all closed up . . .

ANTONIA. Well, I'll open it for you again. You shouldn't get so panicked. You know your problem is that you really don't trust people. You've got to realize that people are OK . . . Well, not everybody . . . I mean people like us . . . the ones who break their asses trying to make ends meet. People like that are on our side, if you show them you're not asleep, that you're ready to fight the bosses, to defend your rights and not wait for the Angel of the Lord to come floating down on his wings together with Holy Providence! I remember when I was working in that factory, making breadsticks. It was murder working in damp heat, but it was just enough money to make ends meet. Suddenly the owners decided to shut down. They *said* the factory wasn't making enough money. They just wanted to kick us out. So we went and occupied the factory: three hundred of us. But the unions wouldn't support us. "You're crazy!" they told us. "You'll never make it! It's a losing battle! Who's going to give you capital to buy the flour? And who'll buy your products? If you don't have a market, you're screwed!"

MARGHERITA. And they were right, weren't they?

ANTONIA. But we tried it just the same. We all put in money. One woman even sold the tiny flat she'd just managed to pay for after years of scrimping. Lots of us took stuff to the pawnshop, even sheets and mattresses. That's how we bought the first sacks of flour. Then we took the breadsticks and we went out to sell them to the

shops. We even sold them in front of the factories; and
the workers saw our courage and supported us. They
made a big deal everytime we showed up and even
bought stuff they didn't need. And do you know what
they did in the end?

MARGHERITA. What?

ANTONIA. They set up a subscription fund among the
workers in all the factories in and around Milan. And
they raised more than eighty million lire. Eighty million!
If I hadn't been there myself, right in the middle of
things, I'd never have believed it. When the workers
came to bring all that money to us in the factory . . . I'll
never forget it as long as I live . . . We were all there
kneading the dough and we began to cry, tears falling
into the flour . . . we mixed tears and flour for
breadsticks and saved on salt! (*On hearing this story,
MARGHERITA is deeply moved.*) But what are you
bawling about, now?

MARGHERITA. It's a very moving story, that's all!

ANTONIA. Instead of just being moved, you should
think about what I've told you; it isn't just a pretty story
about human kindness. Hey, what are you up to now?

MARGHERITA. I am removing these packages and bags
. . . You don't expect me to keep them on me the rest of
my natural life, do you?

ANTONIA. No, but don't take them out here; we've got
to take them to the shed in the garden allotment . . .

MARGHERITA. What shed?

ANTONIA. . . . behind the railroad tracks. We'll take it
all over there, with the stuff under the bed. I'll make
myself a nice belly too. Come here, help me. In two or
three trips we can move everything. (*She takes some
pillow cases from a drawer, and with pins and ribbon,
makes two sacks to hang from the shoulders.*)

MARGHERITA. What's all this about a shed?

ANTONIA. I told you, by the railroad tracks, just across the street. My father-in-law has a garden there ... ten square meters of land ... just enough to keep us in salad greens. It's a safe hiding place.

MARGHERITA. No, thanks, I've had it. I'm fed up with your crazy ideas. Sorry, but I'm leaving everything here. I don't even want one package of spaghetti.

ANTONIA. Do as you like ... but you're an idiot!

MARGHERITA. Oh, *I'm* an idiot! If you're so clever and bright, think of something for me to tell your husband when he sees me again minus the belly and without even a baby?

ANTONIA. I've already got it figured out; we'll tell him you had a hysterical pregnancy.

MARGHERITA. Hysterical?

ANTONIA. Yeah, it's common for a woman to think she's pregnant ... her belly gets big and then when she goes to have the baby, all that comes out is air.

MARGHERITA. Go on, only air! And how did I get this hysterical pregnancy?

ANTONIA. From the Pope. He's the one who always comes in your dreams and tells you: "Have a baby, have a baby." And you obeyed him; you've had a baby ... an air baby. Just the soul of the baby!

MARGHERITA. Oh great, drag the Pope into our business as well!

ANTONIA. Well, one good turn deserves another, doesn't it? (*Meanwhile, MARGHERITA has unloaded herself; ANTONIA on the other hand has built a swollen belly under her coat.*) OK, that's it. Now look: keep your eye on the pan there on the stove, and I'll be back in ten minutes.

MARGHERITA. But why don't you just grab a couple

more shopping bags and take over everything in one trip, instead of doing this song and dance routine about the pregnant mommy?

ANTONIA. Because I'm not an idiot like you who'd get herself busted right away. Look down there out front, in the street. Come here; see that! It's a police wagon. And what do you think they're doing there, so early? They're waiting specially for suckers like you who go walking around with shopping bags to hide stuff early in the morning . . . and pop! they catch you on the fly! (*She turns to the gas range for a moment.*) Listen, if the gas goes out, there's this portable gizmo of Giovanni's. It works like this . . . it lights up.

MARGHERITA. But doesn't it get red hot?

ANTONIA. No, because it's not made of iron . . . it's special stuff they call antimony which goes up to 2000 degrees without ever getting red. It's made specially for lighting the gas.

MARGHERITA. (*glancing out the window*) Look down there, it's Maria from the fourth floor; she's got herself pregnant too . . . there she goes crossing . . .

ANTONIA. They're all stealing our idea; next you'll see pregnant dogs in their little coats, and men with big humps.

MARGHERITA. Listen, I've changed my mind, I'm going with you. (*She takes the bags again and arranges them on her stomach.*)

ANTONIA. Good, but hurry up . . . Even those like you who get so scared they pee in their pants . . . sooner or later they get brave. (*affectionately*) Get going, you big dummy! (*She caresses her own belly.*) I'll go and get the key to the shed. You know something? This big belly makes me feel sentimental; it reminds me of my baby.

MARGHERITA. Your baby?

ANTONIA. Well, actually, he's already over nineteen but for me he's still my baby . . . Fulvio. Even if he is living on his own, with a girl. She left home and everything too.

MARGHERITA. Well, I left home early too!

ANTONIA. I know . . . as soon as they manage to earn two cents of their own, they're off.

MARGHERITA. They're right; personally I couldn't take it at home anymore. What sort of home was it? We never saw each other . . . we never managed to talk . . . and even when you do get to talk, all we did was quarrel, like dogs in a compound. Any excuse to say nasty things to each other, to vent our rage.

ANTONIA. So, my boy, Fulvio, took off too. But pretty soon now he'll have a child of his own and the old story will start again from the beginning; the kids always take off thinking that they're escaping from the compound, but really they're still here inside the fence! It's no good, until we break down the fence and get rid of the keeper!

MARGHERITA. And male chauvinism too!

ANTONIA. Well, let's go. Today really is mother's day!

CURTAIN

(*In front of curtain. LUIGI and GIOVANNI enter from stage left, as if walking along the street. LUIGI takes out a cap and puts it on his head. GIOVANNI does the same.*)

LUIGI. Now it's even beginning to rain.

GIOVANNI. Shit.

LUIGI. Lousy government.

GIOVANNI. They told you on the phone that your

wife's not a patient, so why did we have to go traipsing around like this?

LUIGI. With that circus of an administration, who can you trust?

GIOVANNI. Well, I've had it. Now I'm going to the station and take the train and go to work. They'll probably dock me an hour already. (*He goes; then, at center, he stops, looking toward the audience.*) Look! Over there! Oh shit, what a disaster!

LUIGI. (*moves to GIOVANNI*) It's a truck . . . no, two! Those eight-axle rigs! They've turned over!

GIOVANNI. No wonder, with this rain . . . you brake on a wet spot . . . and pata pum!

(*Enter the POLICE SERGEANT we have already met.*)

SERGEANT. Get back, get back! Keep away, it's dangerous! They could be carrying inflammable material! It might blow up any minute!

GIOVANNI. Hi there, Sergeant. We always run into each other on happy occasions, don't we?

SERGEANT. Oh, it's you. You see what an easy life we have? (*speaking to the back of the house*) Hey, down there, you, on the embankment! What are these idiots doing? Get back, you too! . . . (*turns to the left*) Hey,

over there! Keep moving, get going ... go to w
Don't you have enough accidents at work? You got
come looking for them here too!

LUIGI. Eh, you really know this guy?

GIOVANNI. Sure, we're bosom buddies. A red hot
Maoist. I think he's an infiltrator.

LUIGI. An infiltrator, in the police?

GIOVANNI. Sure. Hey, Sergeant ... look on the side
of the truck, it says "caustic soda," and that stuff
doesn't blow up.

SERGEANT. I know, "caustic soda" is written on the
outside; but you don't know what's on the inside.

GIOVANNI. Oh, you're always so suspicious, Sergeant.
Those are two "International Transport" trucks, stuff
that goes out of the country. With all the inspections
they have, there's no way they could put on a fake label.
You'll see, it won't blow up!

SERGEANT. I know, I know, the truck won't blow up,
but my balls might. You know, what with one thing and
another, I've been on my feet since yesterday morning.

GIOVANNI. Ah, and you think we've had it any better;
"Move it, move it, keep the torch hot. On the job!"

SERGEANT. Ecco bravo! You're all ready to join the
police force ... why don't you take my place?

GIOVANNI. Well, in your place, to begin with, *I'd* clear
away all these sacks that fell out on the embankment.
'Cause if it *is* caustic soda, with the rain that's coming
down it'll soon begin boiling. You'll get a smoking mush
that'll be really dangerous! "Caustic" means that it
burns, right?!

SERGEANT. Right, OK, so now you can give me a hand
... I always like people who show initiative and a
cooperative spirit. Let's go, get a move on!

me and all my bright ideas!
You really do have this fault; you

the rear of the house) Come on,
nd! Let's save these sacks. Do it
for the truck drivers ... You've got to support those in
trouble.

(*The action of passing the sacks from hand to hand
begins. The sacks plop on to stage* L.)

GIOVANNI. Look! Everybody's coming over to give us
a hand. You're always such a pessimist. And they'll
probably be late for work, and get their pay docked.

SERGEANT. *I* never said that the people aren't
generous.

GIOVANNI. Oh no: you just say that we've got to look
sharp since the world is full of crooks and you can't
trust anybody. You know, you really remind me of my
first boss: a suspicious old bastard who had a dog older
than he was—half deaf, but a ferocious watchdog. And
since the old guy didn't trust anybody else, he went out
and had a hearing aid made specially for the dog.

SERGEANT. A hearing aid for a dog?

GIOVANNI. Yeh. A really strong, battery-operated
one. He tied it to the inside of the dog's leg. But as soon
as the dog lifted his leg to piss, he pissed on the
battery—short circuit—and zapp! he got electrocuted.

SERGEANT. Well, I'll try not to raise my leg. By the
way ... do you know what happened to the truck
drivers?

LUIGI. Where did they go? O Jesus! Were they
crushed inside the cab?

SERGEANT. They weren't crushed; they got out.

GIOVANNI. Thank goodness!

SERGEANT. They got out right away and took off like a couple of rockets!

GIOVANNI. Why?

SERGEANT. Because just as I thought these sacks we're rescuing with such love and generosity don't have caustic soda in them, but refined sugar!

GIOVANNI. Sugar? There's sugar in there?

LUIGI. (*opening a sack to check*) Yep, it's really sugar.

SERGEANT. These are sugar, those others first grade flour.

GIOVANNI. The bastards! But where were they taking it?

SERGEANT. The first load was going to Switzerland and the other one to Germany. You were the one who said that these guys never put on a fake label. Real honest folks: "You know, with all the inspections they have!"

GIOVANNI. How *do* they get around the inspection? Don't they have one?

SERGEANT. Oh yeah, they have one at the beginning of the trip and that's that. Then seal it up and away they go; nobody stops them again!

LUIGI. Unless they happen to roll over on the highway.

GIOVANNI. Well, there's always a God in heaven who trips up the smart guys . . . you get what they do, these industrialist sons-of-bitches? First they make the stuff disappear from the shops: "We've run out," they tell you. And then, here it is . . . where it's really going. They're not satisfied with sending the money they earned from the sweat of our backs over the border, now they're even ripping off the food we eat! Goddam bandits!

SERGEANT. Well, good for you! Work it off, get indignant! Indignation is the real weapon of the asshole!

GIOVANNI. Oh, thanks a lot! I'm an asshole! (*turns to LUIGI*) You see what good friends we've become! (*to SERGEANT*) And what do you do, then, besides fucking around with people?

SERGEANT. I sequester! Sequester and confiscate! Thanks to your help, we're saving the merchandise from destruction. Then we'll write a nice report and bring charges. And then, the TV news will report today's brilliant police operation. So the guilty industrialists, warned in advance, will have all the time they need to beat it out of the country. The judge will sentence them to four months 'in absentia.' The President of the Republic will grant them a swift pardon. And that's that.

GIOVANNI. That's that, huh! And what about the merchandise?

SERGEANT. That will be restored to its proper owners, upon payment of a large fine against which the same industrialists will keep appealing until they're allowed to pay only for the storage!

GIOVANNI. No, I don't believe it . . . that would be too much!

SERGEANT. Sure! I don't even believe it myself! I'm not allowed to believe it; my uniform and my rank prohibit it! But it's different for you . . . let's put it this way . . . you can't believe it because . . .

GIOVANNI. Because I'm an asshole . . . I get the point!

SERGEANT. If you insist! (*moving a few steps toward stage right*) Hey, where are those guys going? Jesus Christ, they're ripping off the sacks! They found out that there was sugar and flour inside!

GIOVANNI. Well, aren't you going to stop them? If

you stand there with you finger up your ass, the others'll take off too . . . with the whole truck!

LUIGI. But what's it to you? Now you want to be an informer? You really are an asshole!

GIOVANNI. Oh no, not you too!

SERGEANT. There you are, ideas spread. And why are you getting so hot and bothered about a couple of miserable sacks of soda?

GIOVANNI. What do you mean, soda, you know perfectly well . . .

SERGEANT. No, I don't know anything . . . I stick to what's written on the truck: "caustic soda." It's not up to me to check . . . The inspection has to be made by my direct superior, and he'll get here in a couple of hours. That's the regulation! And I'm sticking to it! In fact, since the regulation also says that "in case of a traffic accident the primary duty of the squad-leader is to place himself in the roadway where he is to concern himself with directing traffic, and with no other incidental duty." So, I'll leave the incidental to you and attend to the primary duty of directing traffic! Arrivederci! (*He exits, singing "Arrivederci Roma".*)

GIOVANNI. Where's he going? That guy is really off his rocker!

LUIGI. No, we're the ones who are off our rocker! We stay here hauling sacks to save the stuff for those thieving bastards! You know what I say? I'm just about ready to pick up a couple of these sacks and take them home with me!

GIOVANNI. Are you nuts? You don't want to put yourself on the same level as those stupid bums. I tell you, those guys aren't workers, they're a mob, a bunch of lazy, do-nothings who refuse to work!

LUIGI. Refuse to work? The "Knight of Labor" has

spoken. But "refuse to work" means "strike." Don't you ever go on strike?

GIOVANNI. Sure I go on strike, but I don't rip off stuff that's not mine.

LUIGI. Oh, it's not yours? And who makes this stuff? Who grows it? Who makes the machines to process it? Processes it? Isn't it us? Always us, and nobody else? And the so-called entrepreneurs, aren't they the ones who always rip it off us?

GIOVANNI. So then since we're in a land of crooks, let's start stealing too. Hooray! The slickest is the guy who grabs the most! And anybody who doesn't rip stuff off is an asshole! Well, you know what I say? I'm proud to be an asshole in a world of swindlers and crooks!

LUIGI. I know; that's what they call the pride of the asshole!

GIOVANNI. You said it! Because you talk just like those lumpen, those desperadoes, who don't see any solution but to hustle. Everybody for himself, each for numero uno! And then, my two-bit revolutionary, all you get is chaos, which is just what the bosses want so that they will arrive at the 'inescapable necessity" of having to call in the military to restore order!

LUIGI. You're wrong. They only show up when us workers don't understand what's going on. Not when we move to take what belongs to us.

GIOVANNI. Well, that's what the union struggles are for. And don't tell me that the unions are sleeping because I'd like to know who organized the campaign to pay half price for the gas and electricity in Turin? The Union! And who organized the campaign to reduce the fare for commuters? The Unions!

LUIGI. Sure they organized it, but only after the rank and file started first.

GIOVANNI. (*ironic*) Oh sure, the unions always show up afterwards, when the job's already done ... Don't you even believe in the unions now?

LUIGI. Sure I believe in them ... but only when *we* run *them*.

(*The CARABINIERI LIEUTENANT enters.*)

LIEUTENANT. Hey, what's going on here?

LUIGI. What's going on is that we're heaving sacks; we're saving the country!

LIEUTENANT. Saving the country nothing—you're having a raiding party here!

GIOVANNI. Oh, look who's here! The lieutenant with a mustache! Doesn't he look like the sergeant who was here before?

LUIGI. Oh yeah, the guy that talked according to regulations.

(*The remaining sacks are removed. As if the two workers who were helping to pass the sacks take off, with some sacks.*)

LIEUTENANT. Hey, halt! Put down that stuff! Put down those sacks or I'll shoot! (*runs across stage*) Yellow bastards, they ran away. (*turns to GIOVANNI and LUIGI*) And you guys, who gave you permission to touch these sacks?

LUIGI. There, you see, on top of everything else we're going to get shot!

GIOVANNI. Listen, Lieutenant, keep cool! And be careful not to trip with that pistol in your hand; because whenever you carabinieri trip you kill somebody. You have easy-trip-pistols.

LIEUTENANT. Don't be a wise guy, you! I already told you!

GIOVANNI. Okay, but we're doing you a favor; if we don't the stuff will all rot.

LIEUTENANT. We don't need any favors ... go on, clear out!

GIOVANNI. Gladly, but listen, the sergeant over there told us to do this!

LIEUTENANT. What sergeant, over where?

GIOVANNI. The one who's doing the incidental duty of directing traffic.

LIEUTENANT. Well, then keep on. No, halt ... wait till I go check it out. Hey, sergeant! (*exits*)

LUIGI. Orders! Counter orders! You see, we're already in the ranks!

GIOVANNI. Yeah, he does come off like a pig ... but look, deep down he's a good guy; he's the one who loaded your wife on the ambulance with the baby and the olives and everything!

LUIGI. Oh yeah? Wait a minute, I was going to tell you something ...

GIOVANNI. What?

LUIGI. It's about those well-planned and organized struggles we've been talking about. Starting tomorrow, we're all on a three day week.

GIOVANNI. Who told you?

LUIGI. I found out yesterday on the train; they're cutting all six thousand of us back to 24 hours; then, in a couple of months, they're shutting down.

GIOVANNI. Shutting down the plant? But why should they shut it down? They're not in a crisis; in fact, they've got enough orders for the rest of the year!

LUIGI. What do they care about orders? If they move

everything to Spain, they make more money . . . and in Brazil even more . . .

GIOVANNI. Because of labor costs, huh?

LUIGI. Not just that; frozen wages, no unions, no strikes, a fascist government that guarantees social peace . . . What do you bet?

GIOVANNI. Pass me that sack . . . and that other one, too . . . and those two over there! You too; load on all you can, and move it.

LUIGI. Hey, where's the pride of being a law-abiding democratic asshole?

GIOVANNI. You're right, but there comes a day when even the assholes wake up! *We* worked, didn't we . . . so now we're getting paid! (*They exit, loaded down. The LIEUTENANT yells from farstage.*)

LIEUTENANT. Hey, you two, where are you going? Halt! Stop or I'll shoot! I'll shoot! (*tries to get his gun out*)

GIOVANNI. Sure, shoot; shoot your balls off!

LIEUTENANT. Those bastards! And they were pretending to work . . . "we're saving the goods . . . we're doing a favor!" And everybody says Naples is bad. (*leaves, after them; lights down*)

(*Curtain slides open, revealing GIOVANNI and AN-TONIA's apartment. The two women, with big bellies, are returning.*)

ANTONIA. Quick, Margherita, hurry up . . . come in and shut the door.

MARGHERITA. Give me some water. I'm thirsty.

ANTONIA. Let's empty this bundle and take another load . . . this really will be the last one.

MARGHERITA. Yeah, yeah, load, unload, I feel like a truck!

ANTONIA. Oh, always complaining! (*MARGHERITA has begun to unbutton her coat, and pulls out from underneath it some salad greens and cabbages.*)

MARGHERITA. Look at this, we have enough salad to eat for a month.

ANTONIA. Yeah, maybe it's a little too much ... but then we had to load ourselves up this way; if the cops in the wagon first see us crossing with a big belly and then see us come back without ... and going again with a belly ... as lame as they are, even they'd get the point sooner or later!

MARGHERITA. Well, you're right there.

ANTONIA. (*Concerned, she runs over to the stove.*) My God, we forgot the soup ... it must have turned into glue. (*She raises the cover of the pan.*) No, it didn't even cook! There's no gas. Those bastards really cut it off! I bet they'll cut off the electricity pretty soon too! (*A knock is heard at the door.*) Who is it?

VOICE FROM OUTSIDE. Friends.

ANTONIA. What friends?

VOICE. I work with your husband. He told me to come and tell you something.

ANTONIA. O, my God! Something's happened to him. (*goes to open the door*)

MARGHERITA. Wait a second until I put the greens back inside.

ANTONIA. Hang on, one minute ... I'm undressed. (*She opens the door and the LIEUTENANT appears.*) Oh, it's you. What kind of joke is this?

LIEUTENANT. Stop right where you are! This time I've caught you! There they are, both of them pregnant now! How those bellies grow! I knew right away that it was a trick!

ANTONIA. But you're nuts! What trick are you talking about?

MARGHERITA. (*collapsing on the bed, exhausted*) There, now we've had it! I knew it! I knew it!

LIEUTENANT. (*to MARGHERITA*) I'm pleased to see that you didn't lose your little one. But you, madam, did even better. Congratulations! In five hours you've had sex, become a mommy, and already arrived at the ninth month ... What speed!

ANTONIA. Look, Lieutenant, you're making a big mistake.

LIEUTENANT. No, I made a mistake before ... when I fell for that little drama about the labor pains and the premature birth! But now I'm not falling for anything anymore; out with the stolen goods!

ANTONIA. But you're nuts! What stolen goods?

LIEUTENANT. Don't try to be tricky, because this time it won't work! It's too obvious now; the husbands go out on a raiding party, then they pass the sacks to their wives who fix up a big belly and off they go! All day long I've been seeing pregnant women walking back and forth! How come all the women in this neighborhood conceived at the same time? I know the proverbial fecundity of lower-class women—but this is going too far! Grown women, teenagers, little girls—I even saw a little eighty year old lady going by today, with a belly that could be carrying twins!

ANTONIA. I know, but it's not for the reason you think ... really ... it's for the feast of our patron saint ...

LIEUTENANT. What's this new story about the patron saint?

ANTONIA. But, of course, for Saint ...

MARGHERITA. Eulalie ...

ANTONIA. ... you know, that saint who couldn't have

children, and then, when she reached the ripe old age of sixty, by the grace of the Eternal Father, she got pregnant.

LIEUTENANT. At sixty?

ANTONIA. Sure; and imagine, her husband was over eighty?

LIEUTENANT. Wow!

ANTONIA. Well, you know the power of faith! But they say that the husband died almost right away. And to commemorate this miracle all the women in the neighborhood go around for three days with a fake belly.

LIEUTENANT. What a beautiful tradition! Good for you! So that's why you empty the supermarket shelves—just so you can get stuff to make your false bellies?! Now, isn't it amazing what the religious spirit of the people can do . . . Let's go! Cut the circus act and show me what you've got under there, or I'll lose my patience!

ANTONIA. You'll lose your patience, and then what? Are you going to tear off our clothes? I'm warning you that if you even lay one finger on us, if you insist on looking, something terrible will happen to you!

LIEUTENANT. Don't make me laugh, what kind of terrible thing?

ANTONIA. The same one that happened to Saint Eulalie's husband, that unbeliever! The old guy had no faith, and he didn't believe her: "What d'you mean, pregnant; quit telling me tales! Show me what you have underneath . . . and I'm warning you, if you really are pregnant, I'll kill you, because that'll mean I'm not the father!" So then Saint Eulalie suddenly opened up her dress and the second miracle: from her belly came roses, a shower of roses!

LIEUTENANT. Oh, listen to that, what a lovely miracle!

ANTONIA. Yes, but the story isn't over. Suddenly darkness came over the husband's eyes: "I can't see anymore, I can't see anymore," he cried, "I'm blind! God has punished me!" "And now you believe, faithless one," said Saint Eulalie. "Yes, I believe!" and then, third miracle: from the roses a baby sprouted, already ten months old and talking, and he said: "Daddy, daddy, the Lord pardons you, now you can die in peace!" He laid his little hand on the old man's head, and he died on the spot!

LIEUTENANT. Very interesting! Now stop telling stories and show me the roses . . . No, I mean . . . well, hurry up because I've already wasted a lot of time and I'm a bit nervous!

ANTONIA. Okay; so you don't believe in the miracle?

LIEUTENANT. No, I don't.

ANTONIA. You're not afraid of bad luck?

LIEUTENANT. No, I told you!

ANTONIA. Okay, you asked for it. But don't say I didn't warn you. (*to MARGHERITA*) Come on, get on your feet and we'll both open up our clothes:

> St. Eulalie of the swollen womb-a
> Bring forth on the unbelieving
> The curse that seals his doom-ba
>
> Black and darken his eyesightness
> Your Holiness
> Saint Eulalie
> Give him a crack on the head

(*ANTONIA and MARGHERITA open their coats.*)
    Amen.

LIEUTENANT. What is this stuff?

ANTONIA. What stuff . . . Well, I never, it looks like salad greens!

LIEUTENANT. Salad greens?

ANTONIA. Yes, it really is salad: chicory, endive, red lettuce, even a cabbage!

MARGHERITA. Me too, me too, a cabbage!

LIEUTENANT. What's all this? Why did you hide all these greens in your belly?

ANTONIA. But we didn't hide them! It must be a miracle!

LIEUTENANT. Sure, a miracle of the cabbages.

ANTONIA. Well, you make miracles with whatever greens you happen to have around! Anyhow, whether you believe in it or not, what's wrong with it? Is there some law that says the Italian citizen, especially if of the feminine sex, can't carry chicory, endive and cabbage on her belly?

LIEUTENANT. No, no, of course, there's no law . . . but I don't understand why you put all this stuff inside your clothes?

ANTONIA. I told you, to swell up our bellies according to the belief in the miracle of Saint Eulalie! We're supposed to carry it around for three days. And whoever doesn't believe in it will have bad luck! (*Very slowly, the light dims.*)

ANTONIA and MARGHERITA. Saint Eulalie of the swollen womb, bring forth on the unbelieving . . .

LIEUTENANT. What's going on now? Is the light going out?

ANTONIA. What light?

LIEUTENANT. But don't you see that the light's getting dimmer . . . it's getting dark!

ANTONIA. What do you mean, dark, I can see. Can you see?

MARGHERITA. Yes, I can see . . .

ANTONIA. We can see just as usual . . . maybe your eyesight's going bad. (*MARGHERITA gropes toward ANTONIA.*)

MARGHERITA. (*whispers*) The light's gone out everywhere, except outside.

LIEUTENANT. Stop kidding around! The switch, where's the switch?

MARGHERITA. (*moving through the darkness*) Here it is, can't you see it? Wait, I'll do it . . . (*She makes the click of the switch.*) There now it's off, now it's on . . . can't you see?

LIEUTENANT. No, I can't see.

ANTONIA. Oh, dio mio, he's gone blind! Bad luck fell on him!

LIEUTENANT. Stop it! Open the window; I want to look outside!

ANTONIA. But the window is open!

MARGHERITA. Yes, the window's open, can't you see?

ANTONIA. Come here, come here and look. (*She grabs him by a sleeve.*) There you are. (*places him in front of a chair*) Watch out for the chair! (*He bumps against it.*)

LIEUTENANT. Ow! That hurt!

ANTONIA. Watch where you put your feet!

LIEUTENANT. But how can I if I can't see anything?

ANTONIA. You're right, poor man, you can't see. Here's the window. (*She leads him to the cupboard.*)

MARGHERITA. Watch out . . . there you are, lean on the window sill and we'll open the shutters . . . touch them . . . see, the shutters are open! (*The LIEUTENANT does this gropingly.*)

ANTONIA. Look at all those lights in the street! What day is it today? Oh, of course, it's all lit up for Saint Eulalie . . . Can't you see?

LIEUTENANT. (*head in cupboard*) No, I can't see! Dammit, what's happened to me? A match, light a match!

ANTONIA. Right away . . . stay there while I get one. Here! I've got something better than a match . . . here I've got a gas burner . . . (*She lights it.*) Look, look at the beautiful flame!

LIEUTENANT. No, I don't see it and I don't believe that there is a flame . . . let me touch it . . .

ANTONIA. No, no, look out, it's getting hot! It's all red!

LIEUTENANT. Let me touch it, I said. An . . . ah . . . owww! I've burned my hand!

ANTONIA. That's what you get for never wanting to believe!

LIEUTENANT. La miseria. So I really am blind!

ANTONIA. That's right, you're blind. . .! It was the curse!

LIEUTENANT. I've got to get out . . . where's the door? Let me out!

ANTONIA. Wait a second, I'll go with you . . . here it is . . . here's the door. (*She opens the door of the wardrobe; the LIEUTENANT hurls himself forward and bangs his head against the inside; staggering backwards, he falls to the floor on his back.*)

LIEUTENANT. Oh, Christ, what a bump!

MARGHERITA. He's busted his head!

LIEUTENANT. Owwwwwww! I'm dying . . . my head . . . what happened?

ANTONIA. The baby . . . "it's the baby who put his little hand on your forehead!"

LIEUTENANT. Musta been wearin' brass knuckles.

ANTONIA. Lieutenant? Lieutenant! Oh shit, he passed out!

MARGHERITA. Now you've done it! Maybe he's dead!

ANTONIA. Always the optimist, huh? He's not dead
... get the flashlight ... (*MARGHERITA does.*) ...
Hurry up ...

MARGHERITA. He's dead, he's dead, he's stopped
breathing!

ANTONIA. No, he's just gotten sick ... He's
breathing, he's not breathing!

MARGHERITA. Oh God! We've killed a carabiniere!

ANTONIA. Yeah, maybe we carried things a bit too
far. What are we going to do now?

MARGHERITA. You're asking me? What've I got to do
with it? You did everything ... Sorry, but I'm going
back to my apartment ... The keys ... where did I put
the keys to the apartment?

ANTONIA. A fine friend you are; leaving me here, just
like that: Great solidarity?

MARGHERITA. (*finds a bunch of keys on the cupboard*) Oh, there they are! But I had another pair in my
pocket, two bunches of keys! These are my husband's.
So he's been here ... he came looking for me, and
forgot them!

ANTONIA. So if he forgot them, he'll come back soon
to pick them up.

MARGHERITA. He must have run into your husband,
who told him the whole story about my being pregnant!
And what am I going to tell him, now? Sorry, but I'm
not moving from here. Now you get me out of this mess
... You tell him everything yourself!

ANTONIA. Sure I'll tell him ... My shoulders are nice
and broad. (*She observes the LIEUTENANT.*) But this
guy really did have a stroke.

MARGHERITA. You see what happens when you joke
around with miracles?

ANTONIA. No, he's the one who was joking around

... I told him: watch out for the curse; 'cause Saint Eulalie's a powerful saint! (*She raises his arms, then lowers them.*)

MARGHERITA. Now what are you up to?

ANTONIA. Artificial respiration.

MARGHERITA. But what good will that do? They don't do that anymore ... You've got to give him mouth-to-mouth resuscitation like for drowning ...

ANTONIA. Oh yeah, now I'm going to kiss a carabiniere? If my husband ever finds out about it ... Margherita, you kiss him!

MARGHERITA. Not me. What we really need is an oxygen tank.

ANTONIA. (*thinks for a second*) I've got it! There's the one from the welder, it *is* oxygen! One is hydrogen and the other is oxygen. Come here, help me ... Now I close the valve on the hydrogen tank ... like that ... and open the oxygen.

MARGHERITA. Are you sure it works?

ANTONIA. Oh, of course ... I saw it done in the movies!

MARGHERITA. Oh, well, if you saw it done in the movies ...

ANTONIA. Look ... you see? He's beginning to breathe ... Look how his stomach's moving ... see! It's going up ... there ... you'll see, now it'll go down.

MARGHERITA. Seems to me like it's just going up ... his belly as well, look ... stop! You're inflating him!

ANTONIA. Damn! I made a mistake and now I can't get the tube out of his mouth, he's biting it! Turn it off ... go shut the valve! Hurry up! No, no, the other way ... turn it the other way.

MARGHERITA. There, it's done.

ANTONIA. Mamma mia, what a belly! Now we've gotten a carabiniere pregnant!

(*The curtain closes. The lights come up slowly. GIO-VANNI and LUIGI on apron.*)

LUIGI. It was a good idea coming to my place instead of yours. At least we shook off the lieutenant.

GIOVANNI. We can't stand on the landing for hours like a couple of doormats. Listen, I'm going to see if I can bust down the door with my shoulder.

LUIGI. It's no good, the door's bolted and there are two locks.

GIOVANNI. Why all the paraphernalia?

LUIGI. It's my wife who had it installed. She's terrified of thieves.

GIOVANNI. So, now when us thieves are trying to get back in the house, we're screwed, stuck here outside the door like a couple of dumbbells. You too, dammit — a crook, who loses the keys to his own house!

LUIGI. Cut out that stuff about crooks! Jesus! Now I remember; I didn't lose the keys, I left them at your apartment . . . that's it . . . on the cupboard.

GIOVANNI. Are you sure?

LUIGI. Absolutely. Give me the keys to your place and I'll go and pick mine up.

GIOVANNI. Sure, smartass, with the lieutenant there, waiting to swoop down on us like a hawk: zap!

LUIGI. No, no, by now he must have left.

GIOVANNI. That's what you think; that guy's worse than a bulldog . . . I tell you, that guy has planted himself there for the rest of his natural life . . . I can't ever think about going home. I'll have to emigrate!

LUIGI. Come off it.

GIOVANNI. Why the hell did I ever go along with this asshole idea of yours!? (*sound of approaching footsteps*) Goddam, somebody's coming.

LUIGI. Calm down, it's probably some neighbor.

GIOVANNI. Cover up the sacks! Hide them! (*takes off his jacket and throws it on top of the stolen goods*)

LUIGI. What's the matter with you? Are you afraid they're going to tell on you? These people are on our side; they wouldn't blab.

GIOVANNI. You never know.

VOICE FROM FARSTAGE. Excuse me, could you give me some information?

GIOVANNI. Now we're really screwed.

LUIGI. Screwed? Why?

GIOVANNI. It's the lieutenant . . . don't you recognize him? You see, somebody did tell on us!

LUIGI. No, no it's not him. It looks like him, but it's not him.

GIOVANNI. No, you're right, it's not him.

UNDERTAKER'S ATTENDANT. (*coming onstage always moving in a rhythmic halting trot*) Pardon me, did you say something? Were you talking to me?

GIOVANNI. No, nothing, I just thought I recognized you.

LUIGI. Holy shit, he sure does look like him, though.

UNDERTAKER'S ATTENDANT. Look like who?

GIOVANNI. A lieutenant in the carabinieri with a mustache who's the spitting image of a police sergeant without a mustache. I feel like I'm in a cheap production I saw once where they couldn't afford enough actors to play all the roles, so they hired one actor to play all the cops.

UNDERTAKER. Actually, I'm not a cop!

GIOVANNI. Oh, no? What role are you playing, then?

UNDERTAKER. I'm from the public funeral parlor.* Could you tell me if Sergio Prampolini lives here?

---

*The two cover their balls.

LUIGI. Yeah, upstairs, on the third floor. But I know for a fact he's not home. He's in the hospital. Poor guy, he's always sick—a terrible life!

UNDERTAKER. Yes, in fact he died. I'm supposed to deliver the casket I left downstairs.

LUIGI. Well, I'm sure his son will come home tonight, maybe you ought to take the casket to the hospital, since that's where he died.

UNDERTAKER. I've just come from there. But unfortunately, the corpse isn't there anymore. I was hoping to find it here, but it looks like they've taken it to another relative's house—God knows where.

GIOVANNI. Oh well, just leave it down in the entrance hall.

UNDERTAKER. No, no, I can't . . . After all, a funeral casket . . . just left there, with all those people going by . . . kids climbing in and playing Indians in a canoe . . . Besides, I need to have the delivery order signed by a reliable person.

LUIGI. In that case, we really wouldn't know what to advise you.

UNDERTAKER. You seem like reliable folks to me. You live here, don't you?

LUIGI. Yes, I live right here.

UNDERTAKER. OK, then it's all taken care of—I'll give you the casket, we'll put it into your house . . . and when the son of the deceased gets back this evening . . .

GIOVANNI. A funeral casket in the house?

UNDERTAKER. Just a matter of learning to live with it.

LUIGI. I know, I know. But the fact is that we can't get it in because I don't have the key. We're locked out ourselves.

UNDERTAKER. Oh, too bad! Well then, I have no choice but to carry it all the way back to the warehouse.

GIOVANNI. No, listen . . . maybe there's another solution: we'll take it over to my place, just across the street. If you'll trust me, I can keep it for you.

UNDERTAKER. Why, of course I trust you. In fact, I can't thank you enough.

GIOVANNI. Don't mention it. But now you have to do *me* a favor.

UNDERTAKER. Certainly, what is it?

GIOVANNI. Could you let us put these bags inside the casket? You know, since it's raining . . . This is delicate stuff, and if it gets wet it will be a real mess.

UNDERTAKER. Oh, of course.

GIOVANNI. Well—let's go, then.

UNDERTAKER. Yes, yes; let's go. I'll run down and take the casket out of the wagon. (*Exits. GIOVANNI and LUIGI gather up the sacks.*)

GIOVANNI. The cops will never dare stick their noses in a funeral casket!

LUIGI. Hot damn, I must say you really got a great idea—where did it come from?

GIOVANNI. The Vietcong. I got the idea from the Vietcong. Remember how they transported all their weapons in the city funeral wagons—and then they raised all that hell.

LUIGI. Oh, yeah, you mean in the Tet Offensive.

GIOVANNI. That's it. No doubt about it, you can always learn from the Vietcong.

LUIGI. Then learn from the Vietcong how you're going to get around that sonofabitch lieutenant, if he's still there waiting for us?!

UNDERTAKER. (*offstage*) Hey, we're ready—are you coming down?

GIOVANNI. God damn, I've just thought of something. The Vietcong didn't leave their caskets empty. I mean inside they carried weapons, but there was always a dead body on top to hide them!

LUIGI. And where are we going to find a dead body?

GIOVANNI. Right here! I'll be the dead man and you can be the guy from the funeral parlor who carries the casket. Hope I don't die laughing!

(*They exit. Darkness. Curtain opens, revealing MAR-GHERITA with flashlight on ANTONIA who is filling her bag with stuff from under the bed.*)

MARGHERITA. Well, besides being careless I'd say you're nuts. Madonne, here we are with a dead man . . .

ANTONIA. Come over here and give me a hand putting him away, 'cause if somebody comes . . .

MARGHERITA. Where are you going to put him?

ANTONIA. In the wardrobe.

MARGHERITA. In the wardrobe?

ANTONIA. Where else? Haven't you ever seen any suspense movies? They always put dead bodies in the wardrobe — it's the rule! (*They lift the carabiniere to his feet.*)

MARGHERITA. Well, if it's the rule . . . God almighty, he weighs a ton — this is what they call dead weight, huh? (*They move the carabiniere's body around, finally managing to place it in the wardrobe.*)

ANTONIA. There we are. Wait, let's put this coat hanger under his jacket . . . like that . . . OK, now pick him up so we can hang him from the pole . . . perfect! God damn it, his belly is so puffed up the door won't even close. Push — help me! There! (*They shut the wardrobe door.*)

MARGHERITA. Look, it's getting light!! Let's open the shutters. (*opens them*) It's raining cats and dogs.

ANTONIA. I can see that. Wait, I'll go put on my galoshes and get my umbrella. (*goes offstage to other room*)

(*The door opens and LUIGI comes in wearing the Undertaker Attendant's cap.*)

LUIGI. (*glancing around, almost in a whisper*) Hey, anybody home? Is the lieutenant here?

MARGHERITA. Who is it? Luigi, is that you? What are you doing in that getup?

LUIGI. Margherita, honey, at last! How are you—let me see? But don't you have a big belly? And the baby—where's the baby? How is it? Did you lose him?

MARGHERITA. No, no . . . Don't worry, everything went fine . . .

LUIGI. Everything fine, really? And you're OK? Tell me—

MARGHERITA. Later, later . . . Antonia can tell you about it . . . she'll explain the whole thing.

LUIGI. Why Antonia?

UNDERTAKER. (*from offstage*) Hey, this casket is heavy! Should we come in or not?

LUIGI. Sure, sure, come on in. The lieutenant's not here; nobody's here.

(*At that moment, the wardrobe door opens briefly, revealing the Carabiniere hanging there. MAR-GHERITA closes it with lightning speed.*)

LUIGI. Come on, Giovanni, you can get out of the casket now. We have to turn it on its side to get it through the doorway. (*MARGHERITA runs into the other room.*)

GIOVANNI. (*from offstage*) Too bad, I was so comfortable in there—I even fell asleep . . . (*He enters, carrying a large funeral casket.*) And I dreamed the lieutenant died and Antonia pumped him up with the hydrogen tank so his belly got bigger and rounder until he floated up into the sky like a balloon. (*The wardrobe door opens up again. Without noticing, GIOVANNI, who is backing in carrying the funeral casket with the UNDERTAKER, closes it once more.*) Incredible dreams!

MARGHERITA. (*from the other room*) Antonia, Antonia, come on out. Hurry up!

ANTONIA. (*from the other room also*) What is it? For crying out loud, can't I even piss in peace?

GIOVANNI. Are both the girls back?

LUIGI. Yes, everything went fine . . . they're just fine.

GIOVANNI. Thank God for that. (*to UNDERTAKER*) Thanks for everything.

LUIGI. So long. Oh, thanks for your hat. (*gives it to him*)

UNDERTAKER. Don't mention it. (*offstage*)

GIOVANNI. Now how are we going to explain this dead man's box to Antonia? This time it'll take more than the Vietcong to save us . . .

LUIGI. Listen, I've got an idea. We'll lock the bedroom door and shut the girls in there for a moment while we unload everything. We can hide the stuff under that bed and set the casket upright inside the wardrobe.

GIOVANNI. Right. Go turn the key, and get rid of this lid. (*They carry out the plan, busily removing the bags from the casket and putting them under the bed.*)

MARGHERITA. (*from the other room*) Antonia, are you coming? I have to tell you something.

ANTONIA. (*from other room also*) OK, coming, I'm getting dressed again ... everything's falling out here!

GIOVANNI. There, that's it ... the bags are all hidden. Push, we have to push them right under the bed.

LUIGI. Hidden, my ass. With all this pushing, we've shoved them under one side—and they've come out the other. (*bending over to look under the bed*) Look at all this stuff! It didn't seem such a lot inside the casket. Looks like twice as much now!

GIOVANNI. Of course, if you look at it with your head down, everything seems bigger. That's called the Yoga effect. Come on, help me set this casket upright ... (*They take the casket and put it in the wardrobe. Without realizing it, they have exactly fitted the casket over the lieutenant's body.*)

LUIGI. O.K. Now what's this about the Yoga effect?

GIOVANNI. Yeah, the people in India use it ... poor folks, when they don't have anything to eat ... and those people have gone hungry for plenty long. They stand on their heads, and with their heads down they can imagine anything they want. Food, drinks ... more, more, more; ... Kissinger taught them to do it.

LUIGI. And do they stop feeling hungry?

GIOVANNI. No, that goes on. That's it, push!

LUIGI. Ah, so they just enjoy the illusion. Is that it?

GIOVANNI. Yeah, I guess ... (*tries to close the wardrobe door*)

LUIGI. You know, after I put my head down, I got an illusion too?

GIOVANNI. I know, you told me.

LUIGI. No, no, another one. I thought I saw the lieutenant inside the wardrobe.

GIOVANNI. The lieutenant? (*rapidly flings open the wardrobe door*) Good thing it was just an illusion. Bet-

ter not let me catch you with your head down again, eh
... Leave that game to the Indians. Dammit, it won't
close! (*fruitlessly pushes the door, which remains half-
open*)

MARGHERITA. (*from off*) Listen, Antonia, I'm fed
up. I'll wait for you in the other room.

GIOVANNI. Go and unlock the door; I can't move.
(*LUIGI runs to open up; MARGHERITA enters.*)

MARGHERITA. Thanks, nice of you. (*sees GIO-
VANNI*) Oh, hi, Giovanni!

GIOVANNI. Hey, hey, your husband told me
everything went fine. So was the baby born or not?

ANTONIA. (*bursting in*) What was it you wanted to
tell me? (*stands rooted to the spot*) Ahh ... you're
back? About time!

GIOVANNI. Antonia! Your belly—did you get ...

GIOVANNI and LUIGI. the transplant?!

ANTONIA. Well, yes, sort of.

GIOVANNI. What do you mean, sort of! You got it,
didn't you?

ANTONIA. Yes, but I mean, it was something sort of,
almost, that is ...

GIOVANNI. I knew it, I knew it. What did I tell you ...
that woman's an idiot—she's at the top of the idiot list!
(*moves from the wardrobe door, but immediately has to
move back to stop it opening*) Did they do a Caesarian
section on you?

ANTONIA. Yes, but just a small one.

GIOVANNI. What do you mean, a small one?

ANTONIA. Well, the right size, I mean.

LUIGI. And did they do a Caesarian section on you
too?

MARGHERITA. Mm, yes ... I don't know—did they do
one on me, Antonia?

LUIGI. How come you're asking her don't you know?

ANTONIA. Oh, no, poor kid, they put her to sleep. So how could she know it when she was asleep.

GIOVANNI. But you mean they operated on *you* while you were *awake?*

ANTONIA. Oh, come on, that's enough! What is this, the third degree? (*Stamps her foot; wardrobe door opens; all rush to close it. Cupboard doors, then bedroom door, all open, then wardrobe. Each time one or more of the characters rushes to close them.*) The coward didn't even ask how I am, if we're alive, or about to drop dead. Considering that to keep you from worrying we got out of bed like a couple of cretins. When the hospital staff was against it. And what was I supposed to do? This woman was about to lose her baby, I could save it. Didn't I have to show solidarity? Aren't you always saying we have to help each other out — and that a communist ought to be a person who —

GIOVANNI. Yes, yes, you're right ... sorry ... maybe you did the right thing — in fact, of course you did ...

LUIGI. Thanks for what you've done, Antonia, you are a fine woman.

GIOVANNI. Yes, yes, you're a fine woman!

LUIGI. You tell her too. Come on ...

MARGHERITA. It's true, Antonia, you really are a good woman!

ANTONIA. O.K., that's enough ... you're making me cry.

GIOVANNI. Here ... come over here. You shouldn't be on your feet. (*makes her sit down on the bed*) With a Caesarian, you know ... Maybe you should have stayed in the hospital a while longer.

ANTONIA. Oh, go on. Besides, I'm fine. I didn't feel a thing!

GIOVANNI. Yes ... you look fine. And look at that

nice big tummy! (*nearly caresses her stomach*) Hey, am I mistaken or is it already moving!?

LUIGI. Moving? 'Scuse me, Antonia, could I feel it too?

MARGHERITA. No, you're not feeling a damn thing.

LUIGI. Hey, it's my child too, you know!

GIOVANNI. Yeah, right . . . now we're close relatives! I'm the expectant father of an Arab terrorist!

MARGHERITA. And what about me? Antonia steals the show, and I don't even count any more?

ANTONIA. She's right; make a fuss over her, too. Quit crowding my space. I have to go out, anyway. (*She gets up and quickly goes toward the exit.*)

GIOVANNI. (*blocking her path*) Go out? What for? You're crazy! You're not moving from here. You get right into bed, nice and warm . . . We'll move the bed over there, near the radiator. (*prepares to move bed*)

LUIGI. (*everybody rushes over to bed*) Stop! What the hell are you doing? Dumb jerk!

GIOVANNI. You're right. It's dangerous, too dangerous to move it . . . the hydrogen tanks are over there . . .

ANTONIA. What is that lid thing?

GIOVANNI. Where?

ANTONIA. Over there. (*points to the lid of the casket*)

GIOVANNI. Oh, yeah; that's not a lid, it's a cradle! Luigi bought it the minute he found out about the baby: rock-a-bye baby . . . It's the latest design; you see, it hangs from the ceiling by ropes and swings—

ANTONIA. Isn't it a bit long?

GIOVANNI. Well, if he grows, you know. We're all tall in my family. Besides, it was on sale.

(*An elderly man appears at the doorway. It is the same*

all-purpose actor wearing different clothes.)

OLD MAN. Can I come in? Am I interrupting anything?

GIOVANNI. Oh papa, this is a nice surprise. Come on in.

ANTONIA. Ciao, papa!

GIOVANNI. Have you met my friends? This is my father.

OLD MAN. Pleased to meet you.

LUIGI. Shit, another look-alike. Giovanni, have you noticed that—

GIOVANNI. Sure, sure, but don't pay any attention to it. My father's a little slow in the head.

OLD MAN. Don't you start that—I'm not one bit slow in the head! (*turns to MARGHERITA*) How's my Antonia! Gee, you're looking fine ... much younger.

GIOVANNI. No, papa, that's not Antonia ... Antonia's over here.

OLD MAN. Oh, really?

ANTONIA. Yes, papa, it's me.

OLD MAN. What are you doing there in bed? Don't you feel well?

GIOVANNI. No, she's expecting a kid.

OLD MAN. She is? And where did the child go? Don't worry, he'll come back, you'll see. (*looks at LUIGI as if seeing him for the first time*) Oh, there he is, back already. Wow, hasn't he gotten to be a big boy! But you know, you shouldn't keep your mom waiting like that ...

GIOVANNI. Papa, this is a friend.

OLD MAN. Bravo! You should always be friends with your children. Now, I really came to inform you that you're about to be evicted.

GIOVANNI. By who?

OLD MAN. The landlord of this building. They sent the eviction notice to my place by mistake. Here it is. It says you haven't paid the rent in four months.

GIOVANNI. No, you've got it wrong, let me see. Antonia always paid the rent every month, right, Antonia?

ANTONIA. Yes, of course.

OLD MAN. At any rate, they're going to clear out the whole building, because almost nobody has paid up for months — and the few people who have been paying have sent in only half the rent.

GIOVANNI. Who told you that?

OLD MAN. The police chief. He's going around all the apartments forcing the tenants out. Great Guy! (*There is an almost imperceptible sound of voices, mingled with some shouted orders.*)

LUIGI. (*looking out of the imaginary window*) Take a look down in the street! What a lot of police!

GIOVANNI. Yes. Just look at that . . . like in a war. And all those trucks!

OLD MAN. Sure, to haul away the furniture. All for free! (*The sound of voices becomes louder. Crying women and children are heard, along with more commands.*)

GIOVANNI. Hey, this eviction notice really is addressed to us. My God, Antonia, what's going on here?

ANTONIA. Don't shout, you'll scare the baby.

GIOVANNI. O.K., I'll lower my voice. It says here we haven't paid the rent in four months. Come on, Antonia, I want an answer.

ANTONIA. Oh, all right: it's true, I haven't paid for four months, and I haven't paid the gas and electric bills either. As a matter of fact, they've cut off our service.

GIOVANNI. They've cut off our gas and electric? But how come you didn't pay?

ANTONIA. Because with all the money both of us earn together, I just barely manage to feed you—not very well, either—

MARGHERITA. Luigi, I have to tell you something: I haven't been able to pay the rent either.

LUIGI. Oh, isn't that just great!

ANTONIA. You see, I told you—us women always get it in the neck. Along with all the other women in this apartment building, and the one across the way, and that one over there . . . all of us.

GIOVANNI. For chrissakes, why didn't you tell me you didn't have the money?

ANTONIA. Why, what would you have done then—gone out stealing maybe?

GIOVANNI. No, of course not. But I mean . . .

ANTONIA. But you mean you would have started cursing me out, calling me a disgrace—cursing the day you married me. (*sobs*)

LUIGI. But did you at least pay the gas and electric bills?

MARGHERITA. Yes, yes, I did pay the gas and electric!

LUIGI. That's something.

GIOVANNI. Come on, don't cry, besides, it's bad for the baby!

OLD MAN. Sure, sure. Everything will turn out OK. That reminds me, I came here to deliver some stuff. Hang on, I left it right outside. (*leaves and returns at once*) I'm getting absent-minded. Here it is. (*returns carrying a large bag, which he empties on the table*) I found this inside my shed. Must be your stuff.

LUIGI. What is it? Butter, flour, canned tomatoes?

ANTONIA. Nothing to do with me.

GIOVANNI. No, no, papa—it can't be our stuff.

OLD MAN. Sure it is! It's your stuff; I saw Antonia coming out of the shed this morning!

ANTONIA. O.K., O.K., it's stuff I bought yesterday at half price.

GIOVANNI. At the supermarket?

ANTONIA. Yes, I paid for half of it and I swiped the rest.

GIOVANNI. Swiped? You've started stealing?

ANTONIA. Yes.

LUIGI. You too?

MARGHERITA. Yes, me too.

ANTONIA. No, it's not true—she's a liar; she didn't do anything! She just gave me a hand afterwards.

POLICEMAN'S VOICE. (*played by the OLD MAN*) Attenzione! Attenzione! Is this the Bardi residence? (*All nod.*) Is that you? (*All nod.*) Here's the order to vacate. You've got half an hour. Start moving!

GIOVANNI. This is crazy—I'm losing my mind.

LUIGI. Cool it, Giovanni. We'd better shut up about stolen goods.

GIOVANNI. Shut up? That's not the point ... We're out in the street, don't you realize? This goddamned woman—this dumb, dishonest—

ANTONIA. Sure, you're right. Now call me a whore who's dishonored you, who's dragging your poor but honest name through the mud—who's played on your finest paternal sentiments, because, I'd better tell you, the story of the baby isn't true either. All bullshit. Here's what I was hiding in my belly: pasta, rice, sugar ... stuff to eat ... all ripped off! (*She angrily pulls it out from under her coat.*)

LUIGI. What ... the baby, (*sobs*) the transplant, (*sobs*) ... Margherita?

GIOVANNI. Oh, no, nossir—this is too much! No, I'm going to murder her! I'll kill her!

OLD MAN. Well, now I've given you all the news . . . so long, kids. And don't forget, always keep your sunny side up. (*He exits, singing "When You're Smiling" in Italian: "Quando Sorridi".*)

(*From outside, the babble of voices grows increasingly louder; men and women yelling, shouted commands, wailing sirens.*)

GIOVANNI. Lying cheat! Fooling me with a story about a baby! (*LUIGI restrains him by force.*) Let me go!

ANTONIA. He's right, let him go . . . just let him kill me, I mean it. Because I'm sick and tired of this wretched life too! Even more than you are! And I'm especially sick and tired of your windbag speeches— responsibility, sacrifice . . . the dignity of tightening our belts, the pride of the working class. So what is this working class; who are these workers? They're us, you know that? And goddam mad, just like us. Dirt poor, and desperate like all those people they're throwing out of the homes right now . . . Look at them, look down there—worse than deportees! (*The clamor grows even louder.*) But you don't want to see how things really are, you want to keep a blindfold over your eyes! You're not even a communist anymore—you've turned into a left-wing church-warden. An asshole!

GIOVANNI. There we are, now the circle's complete! Why don't you take your turn too, Margherita—Nossir, I am not an asshole! I can figure out how things are really going myself, I can see my party's push-and-pull games with the Christian Democrats in order to get into the government. And the workers are right to be so pissed off! I'm pissed off myself. And the reason I'm mad isn't because of you . . . it's because of myself, not being able to do anything, feeling screwed. The party's not here now; it's not with us, it's not down there in the street with those desperate people! And tomorrow the papers will write that we're a bunch of irresponsible troublemakers!

ANTONIA. What's happening to you, Giovanni? Is that you really talking, Giovanni? Have you got a screw loose? Have you changed sides?

LUIGI. Yeah, have those extremists gotten to you, too?

GIOVANNI. No, I've always thought this way . . . except that maybe you're right, Antonia, I have a church-warden complex . . . And I'll tell you another thing, while we're about it: I've been stealing too, with Luigi. Move over — look here, under the bed: bags of sugar and flour!

ANTONIA. You stole?

LUIGI. Yes, but only when he found out they're putting us on half-time.

GIOVANNI. No, that was only the last straw. Look at all this stuff. Now I'm feeling the Yoga effect standing up! But that's not all. You might as well know this isn't a cradle, but the lid of a funeral casket! Here it is, right here — give me a hand, Luigi . . . it was my idea, for carrying the stuff! (*He goes toward the closet.*)

ANTONIA. Stop, what are you doing?

GIOVANNI. I'm doing what I have to do. You've got to know the whole story. (*They take out the casket, revealing the LIEUTENANT, who is regaining consciousness.*)

GIOVANNI and LUIGI. The Lieutenant!

LIEUTENANT. I can see! I can see! (*getting out of the closet*) Saint Eulalie has pardoned me! She showed me mercy! My belly! I'm pregnant! Oh, blessed Saint Eulalie . . . I thank you for this too! I'm going to be a mother! A mother! Thank you, Saint Eulalie! Thank you! (*exits*)

(*Gunshots and cries are heard outside.*)

GIOVANNI. (*all at the window*) Look, the women are pulling their stuff down off the trucks. The police are shooting!

LUIGI. Yeah, but look at those kids on the roofs —they're throwing stuff down: roof tiles, bricks. . . !

ANTONIA. And over there—look at that woman with the hunting rifle—there, she's shooting from that window!

GIOVANNI. The police are shooting at the crowd . . . They hit a kid—

MARGHERITA. Oh god, these cops are out to kill for real.

CHORUS. Murderers, bastards!

ANTONIA. They're running away! The cops are running away!

MARGHERITA. They left the truck and everything just standing there!

ANTONIA. And the women are pulling their stuff down off the trucks!

GIOVANNI. Good for them! Hey, good for you! Bravo! That's the way.

ANTONIA. That poor kid . . . they're carrying him away.

GIOVANNI. Bastards. There you see them, the sons of the people—those murderers!

LUIGI. You finally caught on!

GIOVANNI. Today I've found out it's time to change the tune.

ANTONIA. Yes ... like those workers were saying yesterday at the supermarket: it's a new sort of strike, in which the bosses have to pay!

LUIGI. Sure, 'cause the bosses aren't going to respond to loving persuasion!

GIOVANNI. Damn right they aren't—you can't tell them: "Excuse me, would you mind moving over a bit—to let us breathe a little more air?" No, the only way to persuade these guys is to throw them in the toilet ... and then pull the chain! Then we really would have a decent world, maybe with fewer shiny store windows and freeways, but with fewer corrupt bureaucrats in the government, too—fewer capitalist crooks. And a world where there would be real justice! Where people like us, who've always carried the load to support them all, would finally start supporting ourselves—organizing our own lives! Like human men and women.

ANTONIA. A world where you can notice that there's a sky ...

LUIGI. That plants and trees flower ...

MARGHERITA. That there's even springtime ...

GIOVANNI. With children laughing and singing!

ALL. And at the end, when you die, it wasn't just an old worn-out mule that dropped dead; it was a human being that died; a person who lived happy and free, along with free other people! (*music; singing*) "Avanti Popolo ..."

END

COSTUMES

ANTONIA
Raincoat-light — long tie belt
Skirt
Blouse
Flats

MARGHERITA
Raincoat, fashionable, long tie belt
Dress
Half heel shoes

GIOVANNI
Old suit jacket
Dark pants
Boots
Cap

SERGEANT*
City police uniform
Hat/similar to Caribinieri's
Sergeant stripes

LUIGI
Short welders jacket
Jeans
Turtle neck
Knit cap

CARIBINIERI LIEUTENANT*
Mustache — false

---

*This actor should not be disguised. The point is for the same recognizable person to add or subtract a few costume items.

106

Insignia for Caribinieri on hat
White belt holster with gun
Handcuffs
Regulation book
(same uniform as Sergeant)

UNDERTAKER'S ATTENDANT*
Large blue coat similar to Caribinieri
Hat
(we used firemans gear)

OLD MAN*
Tattered top coat
Porkpie old hat

PROPS RUNNING LIST

ACT I

With groceries,
  2 plastic bags
  3 string bags
One small with dog food jars, rabbit head, birdseed:
  4 paper bags, large
and
  slippers
  tablecloth—Apron
  broom
  2 plates—soup
  2 spoons
  2 napkins—cloth
  blanket—afgan
  2 olives
  dish cloth
  lemon
  battery operated starter
  pot, wooden spoon
Inside coat:
  rice
  pasta
  olives
  bags
Police:
  warrant
Carabinieri:
  handcuffs
  regulation book
  pistol
Luigi:
  newspaper
  keys

ACT II
Scene 1
    butter
    pot
    pillow cases, ribbons, safety pins
    starter
    pot, wooden spoon
    keys to shed
  In Margherita's coat:
    rice—bag of
Scene 2—Curtain Closed
    2 hats
    sacks—12
  Police:
    list of police report
    regulation book
  Carabinieri:
    pistol
Scene 3—Curtain Open
    greens in bag and tied around
    starter
    flashlight—practical
  Left by Luigi:
    one bunch of keys
  In Margherita's pocket:
    one bunch of keys
  and
    oxygen tank
    hose
    ball, tube, cork
Scene 4—Curtain Closed
    2 hats
    6 sacks
    raincoat

Scene 5
    coffin
    undertakers hat
    bags under bed
    flashlight
    celery
    salami
    carrots
Old man:
    2 eviction notices
    sack

SUGGESTED READING

Carl Boggs and David Plotke, *The Politics of Eurocommunism: Socialism in Transition,* South End Press, 1980; Box 68 Astor Station, Boston, Mass., 02123.

Suzanne Cowan, "The Militant Theatre of Dario Fo" unpublished thesis, 1977; Suzanne Cowan (*UC Santa Cruz,* Santa Cruz, CA 95064).

Red Notes, Working Class Autonomy and the Crisis, Italian Marxist Texts of the Theory and Practice of a Class Movement, 1979; Red Notes BP 15, 21 St. Paul's Road, London N.I.

Pluto Press, Other plays and translation by various persons of Dario Fo's plays; Unit 10 Spencer Court, 7 Chalcot Road, London NW 1 8LH.

Semiotext(e), Intervention Series 1, ITALY: AUTONOMIA post political politics; Vol 3 N3 1980, 522 Philosophy Hall, Columbia Univ., NY 10027.

Theatre Quarterly, "Dario Fo's 'Mistero Buffo': Popular Theatre, the Guillari, and the Grotesque"—Tony Mitchell; Vol IX No. 35, 1979; TQ 31 Shelton St., London WC2H 9HT.

——"Dario Fo Off-Broadway: The Making of Left Culture under Adverse Conditions"—R.G. Davis; Vol X No. 40, 1981, TQ 31 Shelton St., London WC2H 9HT.

BELLA CIAO

Questa mattina mi sono alzato
o bella ciao bella ciao bella ciao ciao ciao
questa mattina mi sono alzato
é ho trovato l'invasor

O partigiano portami via
e bella ciao (etc.)
o partigiano portami via
ché mi sento di morir

E se muoio da partigiano
o bella ciao (etc.)
e se muoio da partigiano
to mi devi seppellir

E seppellir lassú in montagna
o bella ciao (etc.)
e seppellir lassú in montagna
sotto l'ombra di un bel fior

E le genti che passeranno
o bella ciao (etc.)
e le genti che passeranno
e diranno o che bel fior

È questo il fiore del partigiano
a bella ciao (etc.)
è questo il fiore del partigiano
morto per la libertà

This is a partisan song, sung by cast behind curtain on
stage, prior to curtain raising.

BANDIERA ROSSA

Avanti o popolo ala ri-scossa bandiera rossa bandiera

rossa avanti o popolo alla ri- scossa bandiera rossa trionfe-

ra bandiera rossa la trionfe- ra bandiera rossa la trion-fe

ra bandiera rossa la trionfe - ra evviva comunis- mo e la liber

ta Avanti 0 ta bandiera rossa la trionfe - ra evviva il comu-

nismo e la liber ta

This is played before the show, and used by Luigi and
Giovanni as they cross the apron at the opening of the
second act. It may be repeated on tape during second act
changes. It is the final curtain song, sung by the entire
cast.

ADDIO A LUGANO

Ad-dio, Lu ga-no bel - la o dol- ce ter- ra
pi- a scaccia-ti sen- za col- pa gli anarchici van vi- a E par - to - no can-tan- do
con la spe- ranza in cuor E par to - no can-
tan - do con la spe ranza in cuor

Addio, Lugano bella,
o dolce terra pia;
scacciati senza colpa
gli anarchici van via.
E partono cantando
con la speranza in cuor.

Ed è per voi sfruttati,
per voi lavoratori
che siamo ammanettati
al par dei malfattori!
Eppur la nostra idea
è solo idea d'amor.

Anonimi compagni,
amici che restate,
le verità sociali
da forti propagate.

É questa la vendetta
che noi vi domandiam.

This is sung by the women as needed.

If we are to link songs to political positions it is sug-
gested that Giovanni would sing "Bandiera Rossa";
Luigi, "Bella Ciao"; Antonia, "Addio a Lugana"; and
Margherita would sing along with all.

All songs are in the Public Domain.

DARIO FO was born in San Giano, Italy, in 1926 and studied architecture and painting in Milan. In 1959 he and his wife created the company "La Compagnia Dario Fo-Franca Rame." They gained celebrity status in Italy during the early 60's from their appearances on a nationally televised variety show, Canzonissima. Fo's political commitment led him to an investigation of the history of popular Italian theatrical forms and also into a dispute with the TV network bosses. He continued to perform in the theatre but in 1968 due to political events in Europe and Indo-China he resolved to stop being "the jester of the bourgeoisie" and formed the company "Nuova Scena," working in conjunction with ARCI, the cultural section of the Italian Communist Party, performing for workers in labor halls and non-traditional locations throughout Italy. In 1970, after some debate, Fo and Rame seceded from "Nuova Scena" and formed a new company, "La Commune," with which they are currently associated. It has been bandied about that Dario Fo is an anarchist. This probably falsely construed from the fact that he wrote a play entitled "Accidental Death of An Anarchist" which relates to the death of an anarchist, Guiseppi Pinelli, murdered by the police while under interrogation. From his own statements, Fo is a Marxist. His political position is most closely linked to the Autonomous Left (Autonomia) in Italy, the full spectrum of which includes Feminists, Ecologists, Anarchists, independent Marxists, Trotskyites et al. Dario Fo is the author of some 32 plays and has had his works produced in 14 countries.

R.G. DAVIS

Founder and director of the S.F. Mime Troupe from 1960-70, he is the author of *San Francisco Mime Troupe: The First Ten Years,* Ramparts Press. Founder in 1975 of Epic West, Center for the study of Bertolt Brecht and Epic Theatre, he has directed various productions of Dario Fo's plays in North America: Accidental Death of An Anarchist — North American premier in Toronto 1979; 6 or perhaps 7 productions of We Won't Pay! We Won't Pay! across the country; a spanish version for Teatro Quatro of New York; and Female Parts in San Francisco 1982. He taught directing at NYU's Graduate Program under Carl Weber, taught acting classes in Nicaragua and directed a workshop in Cuba. Recently (1983) he directed *Breakfast Conversations in Miami* by Reinhard Lettau for Pacifica Station KPFA, Berkeley.

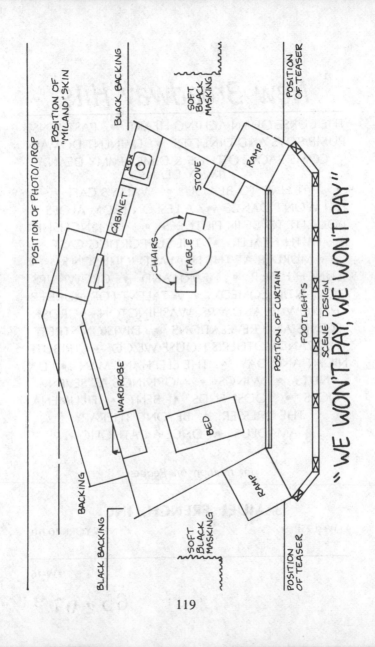

"WE WON'T PAY, WE WON'T PAY"

SCENE DESIGN

POSITION OF PHOTO/DROP

POSITION OF "MILAND" SKIN

BLACK BACKING

SOFT BLACK MASKING

POSITION OF TEASER

CABINET

BOX

STOVE

RAMP

CHAIRS

TABLE

POSITION OF CURTAIN

FOOTLIGHTS

WARDROBE

BACKING

BED

RAMP

SOFT BLACK MASKING

BLACK BACKING

POSITION OF TEASER

New Broadway Hits

THE CURSE OF AN ACHING HEART • PAST TENSE

PUMP BOYS AND DINETTES • EMINENT DOMAIN

COME BACK TO THE 5 & DIME, JIMMY DEAN,
JIMMY DEAN

IT HAD TO BE YOU • WALLY'S CAFE

I WON'T DANCE • A LESSON FROM ALOES

I OUGHT TO BE IN PICTURES • THE KINGFISHER

FAITH HEALER • THE SUPPORTING CAST

MURDER AT THE HOWARD JOHNSON'S

LUNCH HOUR • HEARTLAND • GROWNUPS

ROMANTIC COMEDY • A TALENT FOR MURDER

HOROWITZ AND MRS. WASHINGTON • ROSE

SCENES AND REVELATIONS • DIVISION STREET

TO GRANDMOTHER'S HOUSE WE GO • TRIBUTE

NIGHT AND DAY • THE ELEPHANT MAN • DA

NUTS • WINGS • MORNING'S AT SEVEN

FOOLS • LOOSE ENDS • BENT • FILUMENA

THE DRESSER • BEYOND THERAPY

AMADEUS • ONCE A CATHOLIC

Information on Request

SAMUEL FRENCH, INC.

45 West 25th St.   NEW YORK 10010

#W-16

6520793